☆ *This is* ☆
DAVID ROBINSON

BILL GUTMAN

SCHOLASTIC INC.
New York Toronto London Auckland Sydney

For Cathy, as always

The author would like to thank the Sports Information department of the United States Naval Academy as well as the Public Relations department of the San Antonio Spurs for providing background material necessary for the preparation of this book.

Also a special thanks to Art Payne, Pete Herrmann and Lt. Doug Wojcik for taking time out of busy schedules to share their recollections and feelings about David Robinson.

Contents

Introduction

When *he* gets here, we will win! These are the words that most accurately described the two-year war cry in Texas, where many fans of the National Basketball Association San Antonio Spurs felt they were waiting for a saviour. The wait began in the summer of 1987, when the Spurs made a 7'1" center their top pick in the entire NBA draft.

Why was there a two-year wait? Don't draft choices who make the team begin playing that same autumn? In most cases, but not this time. David Robinson was no ordinary draft choice. The tall, graceful pivotman was coming to the Spurs via an unlikely collegiate basketball background, the United States Naval Academy in Annapolis, Maryland.

Service academies, as a rule, do not produce many future professional athletes. The most famous exception was Roger Staubach, the Dallas Cowboys Hall of Fame quarterback. After completing an outstanding career at Annapolis, he served a mandatory five-year hitch in the Navy.

That explains the reason for the wait in San Antonio. Service academy grads must give the next five years to their country. In the past, players who tried to play pro ball after their military service often found their old skills eroded or they lost their competitive edge to the point that they could no longer cut the mustard in the pro ranks. How much of a gamble were the Spurs taking when they drafted David Robinson?

The odds were in their favor. For one thing, the Spurs knew they would only have to wait two years, not the usual five. Because he had grown from 6'7" to 7'1" while at the Academy, David's height prevented him from participating in many traditional Naval roles. This led to the reduction of his active duty tenure to two years. But there were still other questions that made David one of the most intriguing first-round picks in years, if not in NBA history.

On the one hand, David Robinson was coming off a senior year in which he became college basketball's Player of the Year. Everyone agreed he was an All-American and he was widely acknowledged as the premier big man in NCAA country. Yet even with those impressive credentials, there were those who said a future pro star couldn't get the kind of experience necessary at the Naval Academy. The big stars usually came out of a high-profile Division I school playing a rugged schedule. In addition, David Robinson was a young man of many interests, someone who didn't even play organized basketball until his senior year in high school. Many felt he just didn't have the right temperament, focus or dedication to compete in the rugged world of the National Basketball Association.

Since everyone had to wait two long years to find the answer to these questions, the suspense grew and with it a multitude of opinions. Eddie Sutton, the head coach at the University of Kentucky, said that Robinson "will take a package of skills comparable to Bill

Russell and Wilt Chamberlain to either the pros or the Olympics." Russell and Chamberlain were two of the greatest big men ever to play the game.

The other side of the coin was represented by former pro coach Butch Van Breda Kolff, who was coaching at Lafayette during David's days at Annapolis. Said Van Breda Kolff, "Robinson is a finesse player. In the NBA, he'll be finessed right into the corner." Van Breda Kolff obviously felt David just wasn't tough enough.

Of course, divided opinions can make for fun debates. To the fans in San Antonio, though, the David Robinson watch was serious business. Many had lost interest in the Spurs, a team that hadn't had a winning season since 1982–83. Attendance was down and there were rumors that the franchise might be moved to another city.

The year before the club drafted Robinson, the Spurs finished sixth in their division with a 28–54 mark. In the two years during which he served out his naval commitment, the team was 31–51 and then just 21–61. No wonder the ballclub was looking for a franchise player to help turn things around! So as the time for

David's pro debut drew closer, more and more fans chose to believe. . . .

When *he* gets here, we will win!

1

The Early Years

There was very little about David Robinson's early years that would have led anyone to predict a future basketball star in the making. Many top professional athletes eat, drink and sleep sports from an early age. It's their number one priority almost from day one. David was just the opposite. From his childhood and right through his freshman year at Navy, sports were an extra activity, something he did for recreation only. If he wasn't in the mood or it wasn't fun, he could just as easily forget it. To see how things changed, it's necessary to go back to the beginning.

David Maurice Robinson was born on August 6, 1965. His mother, Freda, was originally from Columbia, South Carolina, and his father, Ambrose, hailed from Little Rock, Arkansas. David, his younger sister Kim and brother Chuck all grew up in Virginia Beach, Virginia. Virginia Beach was close to the huge naval base at Norfolk, Virginia, and Ambrose Robinson was a career Navy man. He was a sonar technician who was sometimes away at sea for six months at a time. Freda Robinson worked as a nurse.

Because both their parents were sometimes away at the same time, the Robinson children learned to fend for themselves. They always had detailed instructions describing their chores and responsibilities. That included housework, gardening, cooking, cleaning and homework. It was sometimes a tall order for three young children to fill, but they did and rarely got into trouble with their parents.

"We always knew the difference between right and wrong," David said of his childhood. "We had a lot of responsibilities, but we had freedom, too. For that reason, I never felt any desire to break loose."

David seemed to thrive on the regimented

routine. He learned discipline and precision from his father. By first grade David was enrolled in a program for gifted children. He showed evidence of his quick mind in other ways, too. At the supermarket, for example, he would have the grocery totals figured in his head before his mother reached the cash register. "David was very curious as a young boy," his mother once said. "He was very perceptive and always taking things apart."

Because of his long absences at sea, Ambrose Robinson spent all his free time with his family. They went on many vacations fished, bowled, and enjoyed other sports as well, all strictly for fun and recreation. As David got older, he spent as much time with his father as possible, watching the elder Robinson as he worked around the house. When he was just 12, David finished putting together a wide screen TV that his father had bought as a surprise for his mother. Ambrose Robinson had to ship out before he could complete the job so David simply did it for him.

"My Dad was the person I patterned myself after," David would say. "I never had any sports role models as a youngster. My Dad was everything."

As David grew older, his interests continued to grow. When he was 14 he was taking advanced computer courses and was teaching himself to play the piano and French horn by ear. In school he gravitated toward math and engineering, preferring them to more abstract subjects like English. All told, he had a happy and satisfying childhood, something he appreciated even more with the passing of time.

"I never realized what a good life I was leading until I began making friends with guys who didn't even talk to their parents or brothers and sisters," he said. "I know now how much they are missing, all that love."

David continued to pursue as many intellectual activities as athletic ones. He played ball with his friends, but never really got caught up in any one sport. He didn't develop an early passion for either the competition or the artistry of athletics. Again, it was strictly for fun, a diversion, pure recreation. David also wasn't especially tall then, though his father was 6'6". In his freshman year at Green Run High School in Virginia Beach, he decided to go out for the basketball team.

He wasn't on the team long. Some stories say David quit the team when he was benched. Others say he left because he thought the coach was going to cut him. He was already beginning to grow. By his sophomore year, he was approaching 6'4". However, David would play no more basketball at Green Run.

Art Payne, who would coach David as a senior at Osbourn Park High, feels that David's inexperience simply made it too difficult to play. "Green Run was a very big school," Coach Payne said, "maybe 3,000 students. So even though David grew quickly, being 6'4" didn't mean much. I remember him telling me there were tons of 6'4" kids. So he didn't really play at all. I believe he played some league ball in town, but he had practically no experience as a basketball player when he came here."

It was in the fall of 1982 when the Robinson family moved. Ambrose Robinson retired from the Navy after 20 years and got a civilian job in the northern part of the state. So in November the family moved to Manassas, Virginia, in the Washington, D.C., area and David transferred into Osbourn Park to complete his senior year. By that time he was nearly 6'7". He couldn't hide in a crowd anymore. In fact, it was his height that first attracted the attention of Coach Payne and others at his new school.

"David came in around the middle of November and basketball practice had already been going on for about a week," recalls Coach Payne. "Besides coaching I was also a guidance counselor at the school and I remember another counselor coming to me and saying that there was a rather tall young man who had just transferred in and he thought I might want to talk to him about playing basketball.

"I wasn't too excited at first because you sometimes get these tall kids who just aren't interested in playing. But being a coach I asked as soon as I saw him and he said was interested. Then for the rest of the day other kids kept going up to him and saying, 'You've got to play basketball. You've got to play basketball.' It was as if he had no way out because the kids were so enthusiastic about him playing. He couldn't say no."

Since David hadn't had a physical yet (a league requirement) he couldn't practice the first day. He came to practice anyway, watched the team work out, even took a few shots in his stocking feet. His father took him for a physical that very night and he was there on schedule the next afternoon.

"After that he never missed a practice, never missed a game and was just a super young man to work with," Coach Payne said.

Unfortunately, that didn't translate into immediate stardom. David already had a goal of attending the Naval Academy, primarily because of their math and engineering programs and for the future it would insure him. Basketball was still just for fun. It was his sense of responsibility and discipline that kept him coming to practice.

There was another 6'7" kid at Osbourn that year and he probably would have been the starting center. Shortly after David arrived, the other kid sprained his ankle quite badly and was out. Suddenly, David Robinson was thrust into a starting role despite a painful lack of playing experience. He was well aware of his shortcomings.

"I didn't play street ball," he said, "so I didn't have the moves, the intuitive things that a lot of kids learned over the years on the playgrounds. At both Osbourn High and even in my first year at Navy, basketball was more work than fun. I knew I could prove myself academically. But with basketball then, it was just a matter of trying to stick it out."

Fortunately for David, Art Payne was a sensitive coach and knew he had an inexperienced kid to work with. As a consequence, he didn't push David too hard.

"You could tell that David was going to be a quality player," the coach said, "but he had an awful lot to learn. Because I didn't know him that well and hadn't coached him before I didn't push him. Perhaps if he had played here for three years I would have treated him differently. But under the circumstances I thought he played well."

Though Osbourn Park wasn't a big school, Coach Payne said they were in a tough league that was filled with some outstanding players, many of whom went on to play Division I college ball. So David didn't have an easy time of it. Yet Osbourn Park finished with a .500 record, Coach Payne remembering that ballclub as about a 12–12 team with David as both the leading scorer and rebounder. The coach felt the team could have been much stronger if David was more experienced.

"We were a hair away from being a real

solid team and the difference was David's inexperience," the coach said. "In other words, we could have been an 18–6 or 20–4 team if he had played more before coming to Osbourn. As it was, he averaged about 14 a game, but he was inconsistent and that hurt us.

"David also wasn't really caught up in the enthusiasm of the game yet. I think that was starting to come toward the end of the season. He was sort of like a dancer who hadn't quite learned to dance yet and couldn't get excited about it. He just really didn't know what he could do out there."

While basketball didn't become a consuming passion with David, he apparently enjoyed being on the team and fit in very well with his teammates and new friends.

"David is a people person," said Coach Payne. "He liked being around the kids and loved talking to them. He has always been a big talker, a person who enjoys socializing. In fact, he talked about a lot of things. There were times when I would give him a ride home after practice and our conversations were really interesting. He just had a wide spectrum of things he liked to talk about."

On the court, the coach said David didn't

even understand the role of a dominant player, another reason he may not have realized his true potential that year. But it was also the lack of skills. He didn't have a real shooting touch and rebounded well primarily because of his size. The main reason Coach Payne saw so much potential was the way David handled himself on the court.

"Even though he was tall and thin, and somewhat gangly, he always had very good agility," the coach said. "In fact, his agility was unbelievable. He was so smooth in everything he did and had the nice soft hands for catching the ball. He was even graceful when he ran down the floor. Those were the things that stood out. He just had to learn all the finer points of the game."

David's intelligence always enabled him to realize his mistakes, mistakes usually made because he still had not developed those instincts for the game that become automatic with experience. Coach Payne recalled the district playoffs when the game came down to the final seconds. Osbourn Park was inbounding the ball trailing by one point. The coach picks up the story from there.

"The plan was to loop a pass to David

under the basket. The ball was right on target, but instead of catching it, then going up for the hoop, David tried to tip the pass in. The tip missed and they got the rebound, came downcourt, made the basket and a free throw. That was the game. Before I could even say anything to him, David came out and said, 'Coach, I should have grabbed the ball and gone right up with it.' So it was a matter of his instincts catching up with his good mind."

They didn't catch up fast enough as far as most major basketball colleges were concerned. As a result, David didn't have to go through the recruiting barrage that can drive some of the top high school players and their families crazy. Coach Payne remembers one game in which University of Virginia head coach Terry Holland attended with the expressed purpose of scouting a player on the opposing team. David played his usual game and Holland showed absolutely no interest in him.

Coach Payne also recalls another game when the team was shorthanded because he was forced to suspend two starters for disciplinary reasons. The first half was a disaster. Osbourn Park did nothing right and trailed badly. The coach was fuming.

"I remember going in at halftime and David was sitting right in front of me kind of moped over," he said. "I came in and threw the clipboard down, really hot, then put on my coaching face and started chewing them out. David just came to attention. He just sat up like a board, like he was already in the military. It really tickled me the way he braced up when I started yelling. It was like the captain is speaking and we better listen. Believe it or not, though, David was so fired up in the second half that we darned near won the ballgame."

Moments of high emotion like that were few and far between. David still didn't have any basketball idols and never talked about becoming a great basketball player. As Art Payne said about high school senior David, "I think back then he would have been just as satisfied being a concert pianist or something like that."

His natural talent, however, must have accounted for something. At the end of the season he was named to the All-Area and All-District teams, as well as becoming Osbourn Park's Most Valuable Player.

Despite these honors, David's primary

goal at that time was to receive an appointment to the Naval Academy. When he learned he had scored 1,320 on the college board exams, David was ecstatic. That news had him more excited than if he had scored 50 points in a basketball game. "I didn't care whether I played basketball at the Academy," he said. "I just wanted to get good grades and fit in."

The Academy, however, might have had other ideas. Any youngster accepted at a service academy must have a Presidential appointment. The academies do have very active sports programs, though and will recruit athletes who are also good students. Pete Herrmann, who was then an assistant basketball coach under Paul Evans, and later the head coach, recalls going to David's home while he was still at Osbourn Park High and talking about the Navy basketball program.

"We talked about the Academy and I asked David why he wanted to go there," Coach Herrmann remembers. "He told us that he felt Navy was one of the finest schools in the country for math, the subject in which he was going to major. He also said he knew he could be successful in life if he graduated from Navy. That was his prime goal and basketball wasn't a part of it."

Yet the Navy coaching staff had looked at him as a player during the season and while they knew he lacked experience, they felt his physical attributes spelled potential.

"We thought he could become a solid running forward," Herrmann recalls. "His hands were pretty good and he could run. He needed more strength and stamina, but that was something he could develop. Of course, none of us envisioned back then that he would eventually become a center."

Neither did David. In fact, while he had all the other qualifications to get his appointment, there was one little thing that worried him. Believe it or not, it was his height. The height limit for midshipmen entering the Academy was 6'6". If that were the rule, period, David might have been turned away. However, there was one exception. It allowed five percent of the incoming class to be as tall as 6'8". David made it by about an inch. Once a youngster is admitted, he's allowed to remain even if he grows over the original height limit for admission. Good thing! By the time David was ready to play basketball for Navy, he was already 6'9" and growing.

2

On to Annapolis

David Robinson entered the United States Naval Academy in the late summer of 1983. He was barely 18 years old but confident in his abilities to handle the academic workload and Naval training that would be coming his way. Basketball was another story. When David decided to go out for the team as a freshman, he wasn't sure what to expect. He still didn't have an overwhelming love for the sport or a burning desire to excel. In fact, he once asked a teammate who was constantly practicing and working on his game why he never got tired of practicing and playing.

With David, it was another story. Even

Pete Herrmann remembers him as a freshman fringe player who didn't show much enthusiasm for the game.

"To be honest, I can't even remember David one day in practice when he was a freshman," Coach Herrmann said. "It was obvious that basketball was not real important to him and there wasn't much he liked about it that year, including practice. I remember him telling me that he used to sit in his math class sixth period and say to himself, 'Oh, brother, I have to go to basketball practice today.' I guess that's a strange way to begin an all-American career."

It would remain a struggle all year. David was, what they call today, a project. He was a player who needed work and experience. And he also needed that little extra that could only come from within. Pete Herrmann said that David simply had to struggle with the college game as a freshman. He was awkward and the coaching staff knew he was still developing, both physically and mentally. It wasn't an awkward stage athletically. In that sense, David was agile and graceful on the court. Rather, according to Coach Herrmann, it was simply an awkward stage in his overall court development.

Another freshman player who came to the Academy the same time as David was Doug Wojcik, a point guard who would play junior varsity ball as a frosh before becoming a starter for his final three years. He knew David Robinson the basketball player as well as anyone.

"I just don't think David had a real awareness of his ability during his freshman year," said Wojcik, now a lieutenant in the Navy. "Our starting center that year was a kid named Cliff Maurer, who was about 6'11". Cliff wasn't a great player, but David watched him and seemed to learn a lot by playing behind him. But there was still no way to tell how good he was going to be."

Navy had a scrappy, hustling team of unselfish players in 1983–84. That type of ballclub is a service academy trademark. The talent isn't always great, but Academy teams are always in outstanding physical condition and play an unselfish game. The 1983–84 team did that to the tune of a successful, 24–8, season. It was the most wins in Navy basketball history.

The team would lose captain Mike Jones,

Rob Romaine (its second leading scorer and all-time assist leader), as well as Maurer and the steady Gary Price. However, forward Vernon Butler, who led the club in scoring with a 14.7 average and in rebounding, was just a sophomore. So was shooting guard Kylor Whitaker, who averaged 10 points a game and was second to Romaine in assists.

One early question about the next year was who would be the team's center? And what if the ballclub had to rely on David Robinson?

Well, the news wasn't all bad. Though David only averaged a little over 13 minutes a game, he still scored at a 7.6 clip, fifth best on the team. He had 111 rebounds, fourth to Butler's team best 277. He also had a team best 62.3 shooting percentage from the field, ranking him 13th best among all returning NCAA players in the country. He had 37 blocked shots, second to Maurer's 75 and was named ECAC South Rookie of the Year.

Obviously, there was talent to develop. David had highs of 19 points against Campbell College, and 11 rebounds versus William & Mary. He blocked three shots in a game on eight occasions. Not bad for a kid who continued to say he wasn't really interested in basketball. Then, after the season, the coaches got another bit of good news in bad way. David was participating in a boxing program when he sustained a slight break in one of the bones in his hands. That was the bad news. Upon examining the injury, an Academy doctor saw something else. He informed the basketball coaches that "there is a lot of growth left in this youngster."

Interesting. David had played at 6'9" as a freshman and most figured he was about at his full height. Yet when he came out for the start of his sophomore season, he was now a bonafide 6'11". There was no denying it, the kid was now a full-fledged center. The remaining question was his commitment. Even in the Navy basketball media guide there was a quote from David that must have made some wonder.

"You've got to be able to balance the academics and the basketball," he said. "It's a pretty good mix, though, because if you work hard at both you aren't going to get too caught up in one or the other. Budgeting your time isn't something you think a whole lot about; you really don't have much of a choice."

During the summer months David had become involved in a weight-lifting program and had also played in the Urban Coalition League in Washington. Summer leagues are a great place for inexperienced players to go to school. It's a street game and a tough one. David not only returned some two inches taller, but he put on 20 pounds and was now at 215. He was still thin, but getting stronger.

Once again David had a full load academically. As a math major, he had courses in thermodynamics, physics, navigation, computer science and advanced calculus. No snap courses there. His 3.22 grade-point average the previous semester proved he could do the work. He had adjusted well to Academy life, though it wasn't always easy.

"Homework varies from too much to way too much," he said, with a grin. "At first, everything seemed unfair. There was no radio, no TV in the hall, no McDonald's on Tuesday nights. But then there are advantages—the responsibility, respect, the security, that keeps you going. You learn to cope and not complain, so problems don't bother you after a while. I also like the guys here. We wear uniforms and march, but we also party."

Finally, it was time for basketball again. With center Cliff Maurer gone from the previous campaign, David .emerged as the number one pivotman almost by default. Though no one could predict how David would react to a starting role, Coach Evans decided that the team would have to use the big guy's assets to the best advantage. Pete Herrmann, who was Evans' assistant in 1984–85, remembers just how the head coach decided to play things.

"Coach Evans practically told Dave that if you're good this year, the team will be pretty good. But if you're not good, well, we're not gonna be very good," Herrmann said. "He decided to center things around Dave offensively. We were lucky enough to have a group of unselfish players around him who also saw that if we got the ball in to David we were going to score points and win games.

"A lot of teams use offenses where they move the players around to get close to the basket. We moved the ball into David. We left him in the same spot and got the ball into him. It was a tribute both to Coach Evans and to David that it worked."

Again the object was to make sure David's

inexperience didn't work against him. The coaching staff wanted to make it as easy as possible for David to adjust so they didn't give him a lot of things to remember. The offense didn't feature a lot of movement and a lot of cutting for David. He played down close to the hoop and looked for the quick turnaround jump shot.

"We didn't want him to try too many things inside," Herrmann said. "Just catch the ball and score. Then, as he gained more confidence and saw that he could score, he began expanding his game and his moves. He began to drive to the basket more, fake and hook. But that was after he realized his talents. During his sophomore year it stayed on the simple side."

Joining David on the starting team was Vernon Butler and Kylor Whitaker at forward, Whitaker having moved up from the guard position. Cliff Rees was the shooting guard and Doug Wojcik the point guard. All five would be virtual iron men. With the exception of forward Carl Liebert, the bench wasn't strong and Coach Evans just spotted his substitutes.

The starting five quickly showed they were a quintet to be reckoned with. Playing in the ECAC South Conference, Navy didn't go up against traditional powerhouse teams, but the ballclub came out and took care of business nevertheless. They opened the season with an easy, 87–53, victory over Gettysburg, a game in which Vernon Butler scored 24 points and pulled down 18 rebounds. This was followed by a 91–74 win over Drexel, as both David and Kylor Whitaker scored 22 points. David then erupted for a career high 29 in an 84–68 triumph over American University.

With their sophomore center providing some surprising numbers, the Middies traveled to Penn State, favored to continue with an unbeaten slate. After that, the team would be traveling to Southern Illinois for a special, four-team tournament, dubbed the Saluki Shootout. Maybe the Middies were looking ahead, but they didn't play very well and dropped a 66–63 decision to the Nittany Lions. Now the tournament loomed as even more important for Navy. Not only would it be a barometer for the rest of the season, but it also might serve to show just how well and how consistently David Robinson was going to perform.

In the first round, the Middies had to meet

the host team, the Salukis of Southern Illinois. Southern Illinois was a small school that played big basketball. Perhaps the Salukis most famous alumnus is Walt "Clyde" Frazier, who went on to a Hall of Fame NBA career, most of it with the New York Knicks. In 1984, Southern Illinois brought another outstanding team into their own tournament.

The game was close right from the start. In the eyes of most observers, the Salukis had a better all-around team than the Middies. What kept the game close was the play of David Robinson. The big guy was suddenly an almost unstoppable scoring machine from the pivot. Navy kept going inside to him and David responded. When the game ended, the Middies fell just short. Southern Illinois won it, 75–72, despite a career best 31 points from Robinson.

So it was the Salukis who moved on to the title game. For Navy, there was just the consolation against Western Illinois. That game did, however, establish the tone for the remainder of the season and the two years that followed. That tone was David Robinson.

Once again, the rest of the Midshipmen made David the hub of the attack. Point guard

Wojcik kept going inside to David and the others followed suit. David responded with an even greater point explosion than he had against Southern Illinois. He was scoring on his turnaround jumper, drives and dunks. When the game ended, David had 37 points and 18 rebounds, and Navy had an 80–74 triumph. Better yet, David was named the tournament's Most Valuable Player, a rare honor for a player on a team that finished in third place.

One opposing coach, Tim Floyd of Texas-El Paso, marveled at David's performance, saying, "This guy's potential is unlimited. He's the best kept secret in the country. He's nearly 7 feet, but he runs the floor like a forward, and he's got that touch and soft hands to catch the ball. The word is getting out."

Teammate Doug Wojcik, who would make it a pleasant habit feeding the ball to David for three years, called the tournament a turning point in David's career.

"From that point on, David realized he could be a pretty good player," Wojcik said. Of course, he turned out to be more than pretty good.

From there, the Middies went on a 10-

game winning streak. The sixth game in the streak was against Lafayette, a contest that again showed how far David had come in a short time. It was a game in which the Lafayette defense pretty much contained him by cutting off the passing lanes and making it difficult for the other Middies to get the ball to the big guy in the middle. In the first half, David had just three field goal tries, hitting two turnaround jumpers and slam dunking an alley-oop pass.

The aggressive Lafayette defense, however, put him on the foul line five times and he missed all his free throw tries. He also stopped being aggressive on the boards. The game was close all the way and just before the half Coach Evans pulled David out of the game and told to relax, not to worry about committing fouls.

After intermission, David began to play more aggressively. He hit five more hoops and the game was tied at the end of regulation. In the first overtime, David hit three more clutch hoops. But Lafayette wouldn't quit and the game went into a second overtime session. With time running down, it was David who again came through, hitting the go-ahead hoop despite a tight double-team by the

Leopards' defenders.

When the game ended, Navy had a 74–71 win and David had 27 points, 6 rebounds and 7 big blocks. He himself called it just "a fair performance overall." But his teammates and coach knew he had become the key to the team's overall success.

"We know we can go as far as David goes," said Vernon Butler, the team captain and also a fine player.

Coach Evans was more thorough in his evaluation of his budding star. "Not many 6'11" centers have his hands, his shooting touch and his ability to run the floor," the coach said. "David can block a shot at one end and dunk at the other. Because this is really just his third full season playing ball he doesn't have some of the bad habits other guys can pick up on the playgrounds. David is still learning to be aggressive and to go to his right. We're slowly allowing him to do more things. Just last week we put in a hook [shot] for him."

In the tenth victory of the streak, an 87–68 triumph over East Carolina, David scored 39 points, yet another career high. There was no denying now that he was getting better. He was more than a big kid with a lot of natural talent. He was, without a doubt, becoming a player. And the better he got, the more interest there was around the Naval Academy in the basketball program. Now, when the Middies played at home, the 5000-seat Halsey Field House was jammed to capacity.

"It used to be that everyone leaves the campus on Saturdays," said Nancy Prout, who played for the women's team. "Now, when the men's team is home, everyone is in the gym."

There were a couple of losses to George Mason and another to James Madison during the regular season, but the Midshipmen were en route to the best season in their history. And they were doing it with an old formula—a very solid team built around a budding superstar. As well as David played, however, he wasn't quite there yet. A few weaknesses remained.

"By his sophomore year we felt David was going to be a very good player," said Pete Herrmann. "One problem he had was his conditioning. He sometimes ran out of gas late in games. It wasn't that he didn't work hard, it was just that he wasn't completely physically developed yet.

"On the other side of the coin, there was a growing genuine good team, and while David was a major part of it, he was by no means alone. Vernon Butler, for instance, was an outstanding player and would graduate as Navy's leading scorer before David. He was also a fine rebounder and his presence definitely helped to ease the pressure on David as he developed during his sophomore year."

It wasn't a season of miracles, but still the best in Navy history. The team finished the year at 26–6. More importantly, they began to show they could play with the big boys. After receiving an NCAA tournament bid, their first in 25 years, the Middies went out and upset Louisiana State, always a national basketball power. They then gave Maryland a run for its money before losing. In that game, David was double and triple teamed, pounded on all game long by the Terrapins. It was one of the games where Pete Herrmann said he simply ran out of gas. But David had made an impression. Ken Denlinger, writing in the Washington Post, described the Maryland game this way.

"For most of the game today, Navy's center found himself with a Maryland player to his immediate left, a Maryland player to his immediate right and a Maryland player hand-checking him from behind. It was the first time Goliath ever got frightened by David."

David's numbers were starting to approach Goliath proportions. For the year, his scoring average skyrocketed from 7.6 as a freshman to a team leading 23.6 a game. He also led the Middies in rebounding with 370 for an 11.6 average. He had 128 blocked shots. Butler, second on the team, had just 10. His field goal percentage was up to 64.4. While he wasn't named to any major All-American teams he was ECAC South Player of the Year and first team All-East. He topped all but one of the nation's sophomores in scoring and led all sophs in rebounding, field goal percentage and blocked shots.

There was little doubt that David Robinson was on his way to becoming a dominating center.

3

A Huge Decision

The more people David impressed during his sophomore year, the more he was being looked at in a completely new light. No longer was he just a stringbean center from Navy, good for a service academy team, but a lost soul in the big time. On the contrary, there was a new phrase creeping into the praise that was being heaped on David from every direction. One example was Ed Tapscott, coach of American University. After David popped for 29 points and grabbed 11 rebounds, Tapscott said:

"He's already one of the top big men in the East, no doubt about it. He's a terrific athlete, runs the court like a deer and he's got great hands. He gets better every time out. He's definitely got pro potential."

That last one was the key phrase. Pro potential. If an athlete at a service academy feels he wants to get out of his obligation and make his goal professional sports, he must leave the academy after his sophomore year. He can transfer to a regular college or university, complete his eligibility (and his education), then be ready to turn pro immediately. If he doesn't leave after his sophomore year, he is locked into the academy and the time he owes Uncle Sam.

With more and more people talking pro potential, questions about David's future were sure to follow. Would he leave the Academy for another school? Was he thinking about the NBA after his sudden success as a sophomore? Even before the basketball season ended, the rumors about David began to spread. The great Robinson guessing game started.

"David loves going to school here," said Coach Evans. "He's a great student and he really wants his degree. I'm not saying it's impossible, but I think he'll stay."

Pete Herrmann, who was still an

assistant coach during David's sophomore year, feels that pro ball had to be on the big guy's mind.

"I'm sure he thought about it from his sophomore year on," Herrmann said. "But he never talked about it much and even when the idea [of playing professional ball] became stronger, he still felt first and foremost that graduating from the Academy would guarantee him a route to success."

When first asked about the possibility of a transfer in the middle of his sophomore year, David gave the second-guessers food for thought.

"I don't think I'll transfer, but I'm not certain," he was quoted as saying. "I'll have to think about transferring because I might be missing a great opportunity to play pro ball and make a lot of money. Still, I don't see myself as a Patrick Ewing and if I spent all my time playing basketball I might not enjoy it.

"I feel comfortable at the Academy. When you graduate, you get a good job and a pension after 20 years."

David's family was also getting into the act. Ambrose Robinson was also asked his opinion about his son's future.

"We didn't push him toward the Academy, but we did guide him," David's father said. "The biggest advantage is its academic structure and togetherness. It's his [David's] decision, but I hope he stays. He's so at home there he forgets to call home here."

There was no question how David's father felt. At the Academy, David was building something permanent, something that would give him positive options down the road. Any professional sport is something of a risk. There is always the possibility of a career-ending injury, or of simply not being good enough to play. No athlete really knows that until he's out there competing.

The thing that was most amazing was that there was talk of pro ball at all. Remember, David had only played organized basketball for three years. It was a tribute to his ability that he was already being discussed in terms of the National Basketball Association. Could he be labeled a future pro star with only three years experience? One person who thought it was on his mind was teammate Doug Wojcik.

"David definitely had feelers [about transferring] from quite a few big schools," Lt. Wojcik said. "They knew he was a quality person as well as a talented person. In addition, there was a great deal of media pressure. All of that made David realize he had become pretty much of a household name and also that he was becoming a pretty good player. I definitely have to believe that the pros were on his mind by then."

The Academy wanted David to stay for reasons considerably more far reaching then simply the dimensions of the basketball court. The Academy's superintendent, Rear Admiral Charles R. Larson, said, "David Robinson is the kind of kid the Naval Academy would go after if he couldn't play basketball at all. He's an excellent student and a natural leader. That's what we look for here."

No one will ever know what David might have done had he been playing longer, or had he reached his full height by his sophomore year and was more advanced in his ability. The telling statement came from David himself. It was made during the basketball season, but the feelings must certainly have remained right through to the end of the school year when David could have left.

"Right now," he said, "I don't see any reason to leave Navy. Maybe I just don't think

I'm as good as other people seem to think I am. But I like Navy. It's a tough place, but I'm happy here."

And he stayed. By returning to Annapolis for his junior year, David reaffirmed his commitment to the Navy. At that time, any pro teams that were beginning to show interest in him must have been extremely disappointed. It seemed likely that David would finish getting his degree at Navy, then would be obligated to serve five years active duty. If that were the case, he probably could forget about the NBA, maybe forever.

By time basketball season opened, David was ready. He had picked up some additional experience by playing for the United States team at the world championships in Barcelona, Spain, during the summer and returned to school a solid 230 pounds. The press guide still listed his height as 6'11", but he was closing in on 7 feet. Bets were he'd be a seven-footer before he graduated.

The Middies looked to the 1985–86 season with anticipation and enthusiasm. All five starters from the previous season were back as were several key backups and a couple of newcomers who would contribute. This was a

Navy team that any opponent would have to fear. And before the season ended, they would show that no one could take them for granted or walk over them.

While the other starters were solid players, especially Vernon Butler, they were still not of the same quality found at the top 20 schools. To compensate, the coaches kept the offense remarkably simple and one-dimensional. But with the discipline of the entire team and the talent of David Robinson, it was surprisingly effective.

"David is left-handed and I'm left handed, so we always had the offense geared toward the left side of the floor," explained point guard Doug Wojcik. "For the most part, we went to him or looked to him every time down the floor. There wasn't a lot of motion to the offense. David just sat in the low post on the left side. We did a few things on the backside with some down screens to keep things honest, but other than that we simply went to David every time down the floor.

"The better teams could adjust to this and therefore had a good chance to beat us. But teams in our conference couldn't do a whole lot with it. Both Vernon Butler and Kylor Whitaker were good shooters, so they had to be guarded. Sometimes teams wouldn't guard me closely, instead dropping another defender off on David. But Butler and Whitaker were usually able to open things up and then we could get David right back in the flow.

"We also spent a lot of time at the foul line. Both David and Vernon were fouled a great deal. David got a lot of calls on reach-ins and with the double-teaming. A lot of teams also tried to physically disrupt his game by beating on him and giving him elbows. That kind of stuff just made us more effective."

Wojcik said that Butler also helped David on defense. The senior forward was about 6'8" and 240 pounds. He played the middle of the zone, freeing David up to shot block and rebound. And finally, the Middie point guard made another interesting observation, one that had a certain degree of validity where the development of David Robinson was concerned.

"If David hadn't come to the Academy and had gone to a big basketball school like Kentucky chances are he wouldn't have been the main man. He would have been one of several. Here, we relied on him a great deal and that gave him the chance to excel and develop."

That development showed as soon as the 1985–86 season got underway. The Middies opened the season by playing national power St. John's in a tournament in New York's Madison Square Garden. The Redmen were led by forward Walter Berry, who would become college basketball's Player of the Year. But as good as they were, St. John's had a difficult time with Navy, or more accurately, with David Robinson.

It was apparent from the outset that David once again had made great strides and was stronger than ever. He had a feathery touch on his turnaround jumper, was clearly the best rebounder on the floor and was a threat to block any shot from in close. Playing in front of their home town fans, the Redmen finally prevailed, 66–58, but not before Navy gave them a good scare.

As for David, he took a back seat to no one, including Walter Berry. Moving with grace and agility, and running the floor like a guard, David wound up with 27 points and 18 rebounds in a losing effort. But he had served notice that he was now a force to be reckoned with on the hardwood.

DAVID ROBINSON

Using the same basic offense, one completely built around Robinson, the Middies continued to play well. They won 14 of their next 16 games, including a 67–64 victory over powerful DePaul. The only two losses during that run came against another pair of national powers, Syracuse and Georgia Tech. The Tech game was a rare off night for David, as he corralled just seven rebounds. Otherwise, he was playing extremely well, leading the nation in shot blocking and also battling for the lead in rebounds.

His shot blocking was especially devastating. David used his quickness, his agility and his sense of timing to swat away shots that most centers couldn't even reach. In a game against the University of North Carolina-Wilmington on January 4, David swatted away an almost unheard of 14 shots. When a center can turn back so many shots, players tend to be gun shy, especially in close, and tend to alter the trajectory of their shots to avoid rejection. That kind of subtle intimidation can be as good as another block. In fact, David had become so great an intimidator in the middle that he was blocking more shots as an individual than nearly every other team in the country.

45

The result was that the Middies had become a nationally-ranked ballclub, an almost unheard of situation for service academies in basketball. With the height restrictions on admission, the odds of a service academy admitting a ballplayer who would become a seven-footer and an outstanding performer to boot, are astronomical. David was a total exception to the rule in more ways than one.

The ballclub continued to roll. They beat James Madison by 31, had 97 points against American and then 108 in a 45-point route of Delaware. David had 37 in that game. The only blemish was a 67–61 upset at the hands of Richmond, a defeat avenged later in the season. The smaller schools and the others in the conference, just couldn't stay with Navy.

David continued to excel. Against Fairfield, he grabbed a career best 25 rebounds. He continued to get superb support from Butler, and mistake-free play from the others. One person who thought the Middies had an outstanding team was Art Payne, who had coached David at Osbourn Park High.

"I really thought that the Navy ballclub in 1985–86 was just a hair away from being the best team in the country," Payne said. "They had David and some other fine players. In fact, the entire starting five was strong. With a couple of more good players coming off the bench they really could have cracked the top four."

They would come close. First they won their conference tournament, defeating James Madison, UNC-Wilmington and George Mason, with David leading the club in scoring and rebounding in all three games. Then it was on to the NCAA tournament, the real barometer that would show just how good the Midshipmen had become. Their first game would be against Tulsa.

Navy went to work using the same offense it had used all year. Point guard Wojcik brought the ball up, sliding to his left and looking for David in the low post. There were few variations. If David got the ball and didn't make a quick move to the hoop or take a turnaround, he'd just kick it out and they would start running the offense again. Of course, if Wojcik saw Butler or Whitaker open, he would also hit them with a quick pass.

But it was David who was the hub of the attack. He responded with a 30-point,

12-rebound effort that resulted in a big, 86–68, Navy victory. Many sportswriters and fans thought Navy's ride would end there. Waiting in the next round were the powerful Orangemen of Syracuse, a team that had beaten the Midshipmen by 22 points earlier in the season. Led by guard Dwayne "Pearl" Washington and center Rony Seikaly, Syracuse had a talented team that could put points on the board.

From the start the game with Syracuse was a barn burner. David was playing a great game, scoring on a variety of lightning quick moves on the inside and banging heads with the tough Orangemen defenders in the paint. Defensively he was playing a brilliant, intimidating game. Syracuse was not going to have an easy time as it had earlier in the year.

In the second half Navy had a small lead and still couldn't relax. The intensity level was extremely high when there was a series of plays that might have been the key to the entire game. It started when David hit yet another basket for the Middies. Instead of admiring his handiwork or looking for a high five from a teammate, as some players do, he quickly scanned the court to see what was happening.

Sure enough, the Orangemen tried to fast break. Pearl Washington had the ball. An outstanding penetrating guard, "the Pearl" took the ball straight down the middle and looked as if he would go in for an uncontested layup. As he went up there was the form of number 50 roaring up behind him. David seemed to come from nowhere, soaring through the air and blocking the shot from behind. His momentum took him behind the end line and out of bounds.

There was a scramble for the rebound before it was grabbed by Wendell Alexis of Syracuse. Alexis went right up with the ball from underneath when David appeared again. This time he came flying in from out of bounds and made his second clean block in the sequence. The fans went wild as Navy grabbed the ball, went on a fast break of its own and scored.

"Whenever I think back about David and our team during those years I always think of that sequence," said Doug Wojcik. "It really showed what David was all about. The whole series of plays with the two blocks was just so impressive."

From there, the inspired Middies finished the job, whipping Syracuse, 97–85, in one of the biggest upsets of the entire season. David played one of his best games, scoring 35 points and grabbing 11 rebounds. Syracuse, in fact, played such a rugged physical game that David went to the free throw line 27 times, making 21 of them. Add to that the blocked shots and intimidation, and there was no denying how far he had come.

"He's as good a big man as there is in the country," said Syracuse coach Jim Boeheim, after the game. "He just killed us."

The big win might have caused a small letdown. In the next round the team came close to being upset by little Cleveland State, the Middies eking out a 71–70 victory. Kylor Whitaker scored 23 points to pace the Middies in this one, while David grabbed 14 rebounds.

Already this team had gone farther in a NCAA tournament than any Navy team in history. But now there was even a bigger game coming up. The Middies were in the East Regional final at the Meadowlands Arena in New Jersey. They would be playing a very good Duke quintet with the winner going to the fabled Final Four. The Blue Devils were

a quick team, led by All-American guard Johnny
Dawkins, forwards Mark Alarie and David
Henderson, and center Jay Bilas.

Yet despite Duke's credentials, many felt
Navy would prevail. Robinson was beginning
to look unstoppable. David did play another
fine game, scoring 23 points and pulling down
10 rebounds, but it wasn't a Navy day. Duke's
speed and the outstanding play of Dawkins [28
points] were too much for Navy to overcome.
They lost the game, 71–50, as the Middies just
couldn't keep up with the Blue Devils.

But it had been a season beyond expectations. Navy finished the year with a 30–5
record, another school best. Butler closed out
his Annapolis career by averaging 16.4 points
a game, while senior Whitaker scored at a 13.0
norm. Butler also had 250 rebounds, while
junior guard Wojcik finished with 251 assists.

But it was the play of David Robinson that
really caused a stir. David averaged 22.7 point
a game, shooting 60.7 percent from the floor
and 62.8 from the free throw line. Those
numbers were comparable to his sophomore
season, though he was a much stronger player
as a junior. That strength was reflected in his
defensive totals.

He led the nation with 455 rebounds for a 13.0 average and in blocked shots with 207. More incredibly, as an individual, he had more blocks than every team in the country with the exception of national champion Louisville. The Cardinals, as a team, had 213 blocks, just six more than David. His agility, leaping ability and sense of timing were second to none.

After the season, the *Sporting News*, the ESPN television network, the *Los Angeles Times* and *Eastern Basketball* all named him a first-team All-American. The other major polls mostly had him on the second team. That's also where he is listed in the NCAA basketball guide. But there probably wasn't a coach in the entire nation who wouldn't want David as his starting center.

Though the speculation about David's future continued to grow, there was no talk about him leaving the Academy. Questions were based on his upcoming role in the Navy. Would David still have to serve a five-year tour of active duty after he graduated? If so, could he come back to the NBA after all that time? Or was there a way he could become a part-time NBA player or perhaps have his active duty tenure shortened?

The guessing would continue for at least another year. David would be back for a final go around in 1986–87. And he would be bigger and better than ever.

4

Player of the Year

It started over the summer. Once again
David Robinson joined the United States
National Team that would be competing in the
World Championships in Spain. At an even
7 feet tall, he was still growing and getting
better. International rules and rough play
usually don't allow for big numbers, but there
was little doubt that David was the main man
on the United States team as it moved toward
a gold medal showdown game against Russia.

It was an anxiously awaited confrontation.
The Russian team was big and rough. More
importantly, they had a seven-foot center
named Arvidas Sabonis who many said was

among the best in the world, good enough to become a star in the NBA. In fact, some NBA teams had contacted the Russians with the hope of signing Sabonis.

This meeting between Robinson and Sabonis turned more than a few heads. David quickly showed he was the superior player. He was quicker than his Russian counterpart, a better shot blocker, looked stronger off the boards and had more moves on the offensive end. David dominated the game much as he had at Navy, leading the Americans to a gold medal victory. For the championships, David averaged 13.1 points and 6.8 rebounds, good numbers for international competition. He impressed even more people, one of whom was former college and pro coach Dick Vitale, who had become a TV analyst.

"Robinson came on strong in the NCAA Tourney, and then went toe-to-toe with the famed Arvidas Sabonis in the U.S.A.'s stunning win over the Russians. [Robinson is] a strong post-up player with a soft touch and an agile, athletic shot-rejector."

Back at Navy for his senior year, David was the center of attention in more ways than one. When he reported to basketball practice he checked in at 7'1" and 235 pounds. He had grown a full six inches since being admitted to the Academy as a 6'7" freshman. As for the team, besides losing starters Vernon Butler and Kylor Whitaker to graduation there was another major change. Pete Herrmann had been elevated from assistant to head coach, replacing the departed Paul Evans.

Herrmann, of course, had known David since his freshman year. As an assistant he had said that he didn't remember David in even one day at practice. That's how he had blended into the woodwork then. Coach Herrmann also said that he rarely heard David talk basketball in those years and he almost never talked about other players, especially the pros. But when David returned for his senior year, Coach Herrmann quickly saw how things had changed.

"I think the better David became the more he felt he wanted to keep improving," Coach Herrmann said. "He was obviously bigger and stronger as a senior and had played very well against the Russians. When I spoke with him during the preseason I asked him his goals and his answer sort of surprised me.

"He told me he wanted to be college Player

of the Year. The year before Walter Berry of St. John's had won that award and I remembered that Berry had come out his senior year like a guy on fire. That's what I told David. If he wanted to be Player of the Year he had to come out ready to go and be terrific. That's just what he did. He was on fire and he never quieted down."

It was apparent from the outset that David would have to carry a greater offensive load than in the previous two years. The club had lost its number two and three scorers from a year earlier. There were no players to provide the point punch that had come from Butler and Whitaker. This was evident when Middies opened against a very good North Carolina State team. David popped for 36 but State prevailed in a close game, 86–84.

Two games later it was another major college power, Michigan State. This time David was virtually unstoppable, operating like a well-oiled machine in the low post. He used his size and quickness to maximum advantage, scoring on jumpers, drives and dunks, tapping in rebounds and dominating the Spartans underneath. When this one ended David had a career high 43 points in a dramatic, 91–90, overtime victory.

"We had a keen sense of awareness between us," Doug Wojcik said. "All David had to do was lift his head a little or his eyes toward the bucket and I'd throw him an alley-oop. Then he'd go get it and finish the play."

The Middies had won five straight before tangling with the Runnin' Rebels of Nevada-Las Vegas. Once again they had trouble handling a big-time team that ran the ball for a full 40 minutes. This is where the lack of top flight supporting players and a bench hurt. The Rebels simply wore down the Middies and won it, 104–79, despite 29 more from David.

Three games later David had a rare off night and Navy paid the price, upset by Richmond, 64–62. But he more than made up for it in the next game, scoring another career high when he tallied 45 points and added 21 rebounds in a 95–70 romp of James Madison. Four more victories followed before the club was upset by Drexel, 83–80. In that one, David had 44 points, more than half his team's total. On some nights, the other guys just didn't get it done.

Yet with the second half of his final

season remaining, there was little doubt that David was the best big man in the country and maybe the best all-around performer, as well. Period. His goal of becoming Player of the Year seemed well within reach. Despite his hard work on the court he maintained a high grade point average and handled the increasing demands on the little free time he had.

For the past two years David was often asked the same questions. First they were about leaving the Academy. Then they turned to pro ball. Did he want to play? Could he play after a five-year layoff in the Navy? Was there any way that commitment could be shortened? Could he possibly be a part-time player? Did he consider himself a one-man team?

As one longtime observer of Navy athletics wrote, "During the past two years [David] has been deluged by requests and demands for interviews by people from across the country. He has taken time from his basketball and his academics, which is of great concern to [him] to meet as many demands as possible. He has answered the same questions over and over and over again, yet maintains his quiet and controlled tone of voice." The same story confirmed that David was besieged by autograph seekers at every turn, in every public place and "he rarely turns anyone down."

It wasn't easy for David as a senior. He was obviously a marked man on the court. Without Vernon Butler alongside him up front, enemy defenses could sag more and more to him. It wasn't unusual for three and sometimes even four defenders to collapse into the low post with the expressed purpose of stopping David Robinson. He was often pushed, elbowed, jostled and bumped. It sometimes left him bruised and battered after games, but he still couldn't be totally stopped or shut down. His ever-increasing skills enabled him to offset any kind of defense that was thrown up against him.

Pete Herrmann couldn't help but marvel at David as he coached and watched him during that senior year. No coach would publicly admit that his star was a far superior player to the others, that one player was carrying the brunt of the load for his team. Naturally, Coach Herrmann did not. But his words show the deep appreciation he had for the kind of person David Robinson was.

"David could have been very demanding to coach because of his status and stature," the coach said, "but he was simply the same David Robinson I had known as a senior in high school. He had grown as a person greatly, but never demanded anything and always gave of himself. He responded to every challenge as a senior from the big games that were on national television to the simple things we asked him to do in practice.

"In other words, he was very coachable. This may sound corny to some people today, but David is a very wonderful person and was just a delight to be around all those years. Even today we try to tell younger players who come to Navy that one of the best things about David was his demeanor. He was constantly double teamed, triple teamed and took a lot of physical abuse. But he always played the game with the same demeanor. He didn't show much emotion."

In January of David's senior year the Naval hierarchy caused emotions to stir in the big guy, because their decision had a direct bearing on his immediate future, as an ensign in the United States Navy and as a potential professional basketball player.

The ruling from Secretary of the Navy John Lehman came as a surprise. Lehman announced that upon graduation, David would be commissioned in the Naval Reserve rather than the regular Navy. The change was significant. In the reserve David would have to serve only two years of active duty instead of the five normally required of academy graduates.

At first glance, it almost seemed as if David was getting special treatment because of his status as an athlete. But that wasn't the case. Secretary Lehman said that David was simply too tall for a commission as an unrestricted line officer in the United States Navy. The ruling confirmed what people had been saying kiddingly for two years, that they would like to see David inside a submarine.

David was aware that the Secretary was going to make a ruling on his duty situation. Once the decision was made, he seemed relieved. "Two years is better than five years," he was quoted as saying. "I'm glad it's over and I know what my future is going to be. I've probably been more ruffled the last three days than I've ever been."

Though it sounded as if David was looking to a shorter service obligation, he was ready to accept whatever the Navy ruled. The shorter tour of duty would allow him to reassess his options for the future. If he wanted to play pro ball, a two-year wait was far better than a five-year hiatus. He knew it would have been awfully difficult to come back after five years.

David's teammates were also aware of his situation and realized their star center was under pressure. Said team captain Doug Wojcik, "It was really a strange situation. David couldn't say a whole lot about it around school. This is an old school where you come with the object of going into the Navy and because of that some hardliners did not agree with the decision. But I know David was quite relieved and excited about the opportunity it gave him. But don't get the wrong idea. At the same time, David was always extremely pleased with the Navy."

The ruling did open up a number of options. For one thing, the Navy also said that it would release him to play in both the Pan Am Games and the 1988 Olympics if he chose. And then there was the question of the NBA. There was a precedent for possible part-time play as a pro even as he served out his reduced commitment. Former Middie All-American running back, Napoleon McCallum, was playing for the Los Angeles Raiders of the NFL on weekends while still on active duty in the Navy. When asked about his future, David chose his words carefully.

"As of right now, I don't know what I want to do," he said. "I really have to look into what details are involved with each option, so I don't have any idea right now which one I want to take. I know it would be tough to play in the NBA and be in the Navy. It will probably be a matter of incentive. Which one drives me more."

David had mentioned that the NBA games were mainly on nights and weekends, which could help him if he chose to play part time. But a part time pro might be a problem. How could a coach fit a player into a system when he couldn't be sure just when that player would be available?

Someone mentioned former NBA star center Bill Walton, who played part time with the San Diego Clippers back in 1982–83 when he (Walton) was recovering from a chronic foot problem. Walton's presence in the Clippers lineup once a week turned out to be a disruptive situation. Several NBA coaches already had opinions on the part-time possibility.

"I wouldn't have any problems taking David part time," said Milwaukee Bucks coach Don Nelson, "simply because he's that good. You'd probably have to sign him to a per-game contract, but you'd still have him on your team, so what difference would that make? Sure I'd take him now and just wait two years to get him full time."

Phil Johnson, coach of the Sacramento Kings, felt a part time Robinson wouldn't be a good situation for his team.

"I don't think having a guy part of the time is the best way to go about it," Johnson said. "He's so good, but maybe you'd have to bite the bullet and wait for him. Sure, you could try being flexible and see how things went, but my feeling is that as a part time player it would be somewhat disruptive."

There was little doubt that nearly every coach in the NBA had David at the top of their list. Outstanding centers are always at a premium, so the wheels had to be spinning in most NBA towns when the change in David's duty time was announced. David knew it wouldn't be easy if he tried to go the part-time route.

"The NBA is definitely a full-time job," he

said. "It would be tough to play and serve in the Navy at the same time. But I also think that playing part time would get me used to the scenery, the whole life style for two years. The team I was on just couldn't worry about me contributing that much. They would be priming for the third year, when I'm discharged."

David also knew that some people would continue to look at the ruling as a special concession to a star athlete. He didn't believe it was that way. "I always felt the Navy would be fair and consider what's best for me and what's best for them," he said. "I feel as if that's pretty much what has happened. Some people are going to be upset, feeling like they're making concessions for me. But half the people are going to be glad for me because they feel I'm gifted and it's not my fault that I've grown."

Once the excitement of the Navy decision had died down everyone began to realize that there was still half a season to play. Now they had to wonder if David's mind would still be focused on basketball and not the distractions.

After the loss to Drexel, the Middies bounced back to beat an outgunned William & Mary quintet. Next they had another big test, this one against the University of Kentucky, a school where basketball legends are almost as common as the thoroughbred horses that are raised there. The thought of a Kentucky team losing a game to the Naval Academy would have been enough to cause the legendary Wildcat coach, Adolph Rupp, to turn over in his grave.

It didn't happen, though when the game was over, it was obvious that no combination of Wildcats could tame David Robinson. The big guy equalled his career high by scoring 45 points in an 80–69 defeat. He also grabbed 14 rebounds, blocked 10 shots, and again proved himself the best player on the court. He did it this time before a national television audience.

In the next game against UNC-Wilmington, David only scored 23, but it was his clutch jump shot in the last second that gave Navy a 67–66 victory. And two games later against James Madison, David threw up a last-second, 42-foot desperation shot that got nothing but net for yet another winning hoop. Plain and simply, he was doing it all.

"David made just an unbelievable shot against James Madison," said Pete Herrmann.

"But he was always clutch and wanted the ball when the game was on the line. Those are the biggest things you remember as a coach."

With Robinson leading the way, Navy began putting it together. After the loss to Kentucky, the Midshipmen won 13 straight games. Three of these wins were in the conference tournament and the Middies were the Colonial Athletic Association champions. (The Conference had been reorganized from the ECAC South the year before.) Once again the team was in the NCAA tournament, coming into the tourney with a record of 26–5, their fourth straight 20-win season.

"We knew it wouldn't be easy this time," Coach Herrmann said. "We had to face Michigan in the first round and if we won that we'd probably had to go against North Carolina. It was a tough seed."

The NCAA East Regional game was played at Charlotte, North Carolina. The Wolverines had the type of team that always gave Navy trouble. They ran the ball and constantly pushed it up the floor. Michigan had no desire to get into a half court game with Navy. In a half court game, David could easily dominate at both ends of the floor.

Fifteen minutes before game time, Coach Herrmann was in the locker room, sitting with David. The average athlete would be focused in, concentrating on the upcoming ballgame. David looked at his coach and when he started to speak, Pete Herrmann figured it would be something about the game.

"Instead of saying something about the game, David suddenly asks me, 'Coach, have you ever tried Tae Kwon Do?' That was a form of martial arts that he was studying. I was shocked. I just said, 'What, Dave?' And he said, 'I'm into it now and it's great. It really helps me a lot.' And here I'm thinking, we're 15 minutes from taking the floor against Michigan. Why is he telling me this now? He's got to be kidding. But that was David. He loved the challenge of new things and his mind was always occupied with something."

The contest against Michigan would turn out to be David's final game as a collegian and it's hard to envision a player going out in finer style, even in a losing effort. The Michigan pressure was simply too much for the Middies. Navy did what it had been doing for three years, looked inside to get the ball to David. When they did, he nearly performed miracles with it, using his entire repertoire of moves and shots to score again and again.

When it ended, however, the Spartans had a 97–82 victory but the standing ovation at Charlotte was mainly for David Robinson. The big guy had bowed out with a career best 50 points in an absolutely brilliant effort that had to convince the few remaining doubters that this 7'1" dynamo was the real thing. David hit 22 of 37 field goal tries en route to his 50-point night.

Once the smoke of the final defeat had cleared it became even more apparent what a great career David had carved out at the Naval Academy. He finished his senior year with 903 points and a 28.2 scoring average, third best among Division I players in the country. He averaged 11.8 rebounds a game, fourth best in the country and his 144 blocks for a 4.5 average was again tops in the land.

Interestingly enough, David's scoring average was up, but his rebounds and blocks down from his junior year. But according to Pete Herrmann, it wasn't indicative of any falloff in his play.

"The blocks were probably down because teams just stopped taking it inside against him," the coach said. "They saw what happened the year before and he still led the nation. Part of the reason his rebounds were down some was probably because he was asked to carry more of a load on the offensive end. There no doubt that he just got better and better, every year he was here."

Needless to say, David also set a slew of Naval Academy records. He passed Vernon Butler as the Academy's all-time leading scorer and was also the career leader in rebounding and blocked shots. His 2,669 career points were 10th best in NCAA history. He was also the career leader in blocked shots (516) in NCAA annals, setting a record for a season (207) and a single game (14). He had 30, 30-point games during his career, including 15 in his senior year alone.

To no one's surprise, David became an All-American. Not to name him at the starting center spot would be tantamount to lunacy. He also realized the goal he had stated to Pete Herrmann before the season began. Shortly after the season ended, David Robinson was named college basketball's Player of the Year.

5

The Center of Attention

David graduated from the United States Naval Academy in June of 1987 with a bachelor's degree in mathematics. He immediately became Ensign David Robinson. In early July he was scheduled to report to the Navy submarine base at Kings Bay, Georgia, where he would be the assistant resident officer in charge of construction. His salary from the Navy would be a modest $315.23 a week.

But before David would report to Kings Bay, there was another matter to be settled. The National Basketball draft was coming up and it was a question whether a team would use a high draft choice to pick David. Picking David would not pay any immediate dividends. He couldn't even be a part time player. There was a new Secretary of the Navy who ruled that David would not be able to play any professional ball while serving his two-year tour of duty. A team picking David would be looking three years down the road.

Drafting David in 1987 was a risk for other reasons, as well. If David chose not to sign with the drafting team, he could reenter the draft in 1988 and decide if he wanted to sign with the team that picked him then. If he chose not to sign again, he would again be eligible for the draft in '89. The ball was in his court. He was in the driver's seat.

"It's a great option to say that two years from now I can play with whomever I want," David said. "The big factor for me is my comfort level. I realize that wherever I go there's going to be something I don't like, whether it's the traffic on the freeways or the smog during the summer."

As usual, David was keeping his options open. He was as interested as everyone else when the lower-echelon NBA teams gathered in New York to determined which had the number one pick. The so-called draft lottery determines the order of the first seven picks by random selection. Any one of the seven teams can get the rights for the first pick. In 1987, that team was the San Antonio Spurs.

The Spurs didn't waste any time. Without hesitation, they made David Robinson the number one choice in the 1987 NBA draft. Could they sign him? Would San Antonio qualify as a place David would feel comfortable? That was the question asked soon after the pick was announced. David remained non-committal. He would continue to weigh his options.

"I just want to relax and enjoy my experience in the Navy," he said.

As for the Spurs, they were a team that desperately needed a dominant player. The franchise had started in Dallas as part of the maverick American Basketball Association in 1967. In 1973 the club moved to San Antonio, but the still young ABA was struggling, unable to achieve the stability of the older, established National Basketball Association. Then, after the 1975–76 season the ABA folded for good.

A year later, the Spurs were one of four ABA teams taken into the NBA (the others were the New York Nets, Denver and Indiana). San Antonio surprised many people by producing a winning team in their first NBA season, finishing at 44–38. They also had a budding star in guard George Gervin, who averaged 23.1 points a game, played in the NBA All-Star Game and was named to the all-NBA second team.

In 1977–78, the Spurs won their division with a 52–30 mark. Gervin took the league scoring crown with a 27.2 average. They also got outstanding play from forward Larry Kenon, guard Mike Gale and center Billy Paultz. The Spurs had brought a talented group to the NBA, but one that was a notch or so beneath championship caliber.

The club took three straight conference titles in 1978–79, 1980–81 and 1982–83. Gervin was still the big star. The 1982–83 team also received major contributions from forward Mike Mitchell, center Artis Gilmore, forward Gene Banks and guard Johnny Moore. In the playoffs, the team went all the way to the Western Division finals before losing to the Los Angeles Lakers.

After that, things began going downhill. By 1986–87 the club was last in its division with a 28–54 mark, their worst ever. Attendance was at its lowest ebb since back in 1975–76 and had been dropping every year since 1978–79. Talk of moving the franchise was in the air. Despite the drafting of All-American guard Johnny Dawkins out of Duke the year before, the team was basically faceless and without a strong identity. For these reasons the drafting of David Robinson was a necessity, although there was no guarantee of signing him.

David made it clear he was going to take his time before making a decision. He reported to Kings Bay where he did his Navy job with his usual efficiency. Late in the summer he was given leave to play with the United States team in the Pan Am Games. With Robinson in the lineup the U.S. was considered a shoe-in for a gold medal: But when the team was upset by Brazil in the final, the critics came out of the woodwork, complaining that David hadn't played with his usual verve and fire. Maybe he was just rusty.

Meanwhile, negotiations with the Spurs continued. It would take a sizable contract with built-in security for David to sign. Finally, in November, the announcement came out of San Antonio. The deal was done. David had signed with the Spurs to begin play in the 1989–90 season. The contract was a whopper, a $26 million pact spread over eight years. Now he was one of the highest paid players in team sports, and he also had the security he wanted with the eight year deal.

To some, the signing was a shock. San Antonio seemed little more than a laid back south Texas town with a large Mexican-American population, not the kind of city where an athlete of David's all-around potential and worldly interests should perform. They thought he would do better a high-profile, high-visibility city like New York or Los Angeles, where he could be a media star as well as a top athlete. But that just wasn't David Robinson.

"David needs San Antonio at this point in his life," his father was quoted as saying. And David himself said he would rather grow in a relaxed city than to have the pressure of a large and bustling media-oriented metropolis. He was basically a quiet person and a careful one. He still preferred staying at home, seeing friends, tinkering with his computers or playing his music as opposed to always going out on the town.

"You've got to be smart and choose how to have fun," he once said. "People make a conscious choice to do things like drugs."

So David had no qualms about signing with San Antonio. The Spurs would still have nearly two years to wait, but the city celebrated the signing. There were many knowledgeable and very enthusiastic fans who were disappointed in the way the team had deteriorated during the past several years. When George Gervin was an acknowledged superstar and the club was winning in the late 1970s and early 1980s, attendance was good and the Spurs had a loyal following. Now the city desperately wanted another winner.

Everyone would have loved it if David joined the team with the other draft choices for the 1987–88 season. But that was impossible. Without David, the Spurs struggled through a 31–51 campaign, barely making the playoffs before losing to the Lakers in three straight. Greg "Cadillac" Anderson, the team's other first round choice, was on the NBA All-Rookie Team and was runner-up in the Rookie of the Year balloting. Veteran guard Alvin Robertson was the club's leading scorer (19.6) and was chosen to the NBA's All-Defensive second team.

Johnny Dawkins played well, as did Walter Berry, who had preceded David as college Player of the Year. The ballclub still didn't have a first-rate center.

Then, in the summer of 1988, David got permission from the Navy to try out for the United States Olympic team. Again, everyone assumed that just his presence on the team meant a gold medal. But reality was not up to expectations and doubts surfaced again as to whether David would step into the NBA and be an instant star.

He wasn't playing with any real passion in the early warm-up and practice games. The team went on a tour of Europe in June and began winning easily, defeating an assortment of teams from other countries by an average score of 104–67. Playing an Austrian team at the end of June, for example, the United States won in a walk, 115–46. In that one, David had 9 points and 7 rebounds in just 12 minutes of action. Maybe it was the caliber of the competition, but he looked almost bored.

Then there was a contest against the French national team. Again the U.S. won it, 100–82, but Dave almost appeared to be elsewhere. He had four points, four fouls and four turnovers in 19 minutes on the floor. You couldn't even call it action.

"Traditionally, I've not done well against lesser competition," David said. "But the one thing this series of games has shown me is how far I have to go and in what areas I'm hurting. My offense is way behind and I need to go to the basket more."

But a look at the recent past raised even more questions. Several months earlier, in March, David was playing for a Navy team in an armed forces tournament. With the future Spur in the lineup, the Navy team was supposed to win easily. Instead, they were trounced by a smaller Army squad, 118–71. David had played for just 16 minutes and looked very bad. St. Peter's College athletic director, Bill Stein, who was also an Olympic team assistant, saw the game and said, "David couldn't get down the court three times in a row."

It was apparent that David was not in playing condition. Part of the reason for the European tour was to allow him to work himself back into game shape. Even teammate Steve Kerr sounded worried about the whole situation.

"Dave's so rusty and doesn't act like he's

into the games at all," Kerr said. "I don't see how this tour does the rest of us much good because the competition is so ridiculous. But the whole trip was supposed to be for David and that kind of worries us."

George Raveling of the University of Southern California, who was also an assistant coach under Georgetown's John Thompson, said that David had to prove himself and make the team, just like everyone else.

"Nobody is a lock yet," said Raveling. "Many people think Robinson had the team made before this trip. I didn't share that view. David hasn't play with intensity like we want him to or dominated like he can. Great centers lead teams to championships because they play hard every minute. It's not fair to the other players to give him minutes at their expense when he isn't playing up to his ability."

It wasn't easy for David to keep himself in game condition while serving in the Navy. It was also tough to keep all the skills sharp playing only in service games. Remember, David had played just five years of organized basketball. He was not only still learning about the sport, but also about his own physical abilities.

Then came a game with a strong team from Spain. Suddenly, David looked like the Robinson of old, the guy who had been so dominant at Navy the past two years. He scored 13 points and collected 7 rebounds in the first half alone, eventually winding up with an 18-point, 9-rebound night. He swept the boards with what appeared to be the wingspan of a condor, flew through the air and slam-dunked at the other end, and also showed his old touch with some soft, turnaround jumpers.

"Gee, I guess he just needed somebody good to play against," said Steve Kerr, afterward.

George Raveling's reaction was simple. "All the questions have been answered," the assistant coach said.

Only David still had reservations. He knew he still wasn't playing to his potential.

"I didn't feel that far behind at the Olympic trials," he said, "but the more I play and the more I see about myself, the more I notice deficiencies that I'd rather not talk about. I'm only 70 percent of where I want to be."

Maybe David saw it coming. He didn't

regain the form that had made him the best
college player in the land. In addition, the
remainder of the United States squad wasn't
up to the standard of some Olympic teams of
the past. The result was a third place finish
at the Los Angeles Olympiad, the worst U.S.
showing ever. David averaged only 12 points
and 6 rebounds during the Games, way below
his Navy standards. Couple that with the U.S.
defeat and the fingers pointed once again.

As George Raveling had said, great centers
win championships. There were many who
believed that and felt that David's less-than-
stellar play cost the U.S. the gold medal. In
addition, he still had to spend another year in
the Navy before joining the Spurs. If he had
fallen back so much in just a year, what would
he be like after another 12 months had passed?

6

Getting Ready to Rumble

While David was trying to regain his form with the Olympic team, there were major changes made in San Antonio. In the spring of 1988 the franchise was sold with the stipulation that it remain in San Antonio. New owner Red McCombs was committed to building a winner, and in the summer took the first step toward reorganizing the team by hiring Larry Brown as his new head coach.

Most basketball fans were familiar with the Brown odyssey. He was known as a traveling man, a coach who couldn't stay in one place for too long. After a successful stint as a college and professional player, Brown

began his coaching career in 1972 with the
Carolina franchise in the young American
Basketball Association. Two years later he
moved to Denver of the ABA. Then there were
two years as the head man at UCLA, where he
took his first club to a surprising spot in the
national championship game. Although the
Bruins lost, Brown was looked upon as almost
a miracle man.

After that, Brown went to the New Jersey
Nets of the NBA, his tenure lasting just two
years. Again, he was lured back to the college
ranks, taking over the Kansas Jayhawks in
1983 and coaching there for five years culmi-
nating in a National Championship in 1988.
With the college world at his feet the unpre-
dictable Brown decided to take up a new
challenge, that of rebuilding the Spurs.

Why hire a coach who has shown a pen-
chant for moving on? Yes, Brown had shuffled
around a lot, looking for new challenges.
However, there was one constant. Wherever
he landed and wherever he coached, Larry
Brown emerged a winner. There had not been
a single losing season in 16 years of coaching.
His 629–330 combined coaching record was
outstanding. So why not Brown?

The 1988–89 season would turn out to be the toughest of Larry Brown's coaching career. Nothing went right from the start, except perhaps the play of first round draft pick Willie Anderson of Georgia. Anderson became the team's leading scorer with an 18.6 average and would eventually be runner-up in the Rookie of the Year balloting.

On the down side, guard Johnny Dawkins suffered a nerve injury that would keep him out of 51 of the team's final 59 games. In late January, guard Alvin Robertson sprained his knee and would miss some 17 games. Only Vernon Maxwell, Greg Anderson and Willie Anderson were able to play what amounted to a full schedule. There were numerous personnel changes during the season and still no big man in the middle. Greg Anderson was the team's leading rebounder with just 676 caroms.

As a result this was the worst season in franchise history, a 21–61 record that saw the team top only the expansionist Miami Heat in the Midwest Division of the Western Conference. On top of that was the knowledge of David's less than stellar play in the Olympics. Was it added reason to worry? Not to the average fan, to the man on the street in San Antonio David was still looked upon as a franchise saviour.

When *he* gets here, we will win!

Beginning in May of 1989, Coach Brown and his staff began making preparations for David's arrival and for the 1989–90 season. David's discharge date from the Navy was May 19. Upon his release David went to work getting ready for the basketball season. His target date was the November 4, opener against the Los Angeles Lakers.

"I will be so nervous when that day comes," David said. "Nervousness always shows up in my leg and my right leg will probably be going about 100 miles an hour that afternoon. I'll be so hyped up. Let's say I'm already feeling the anticipation."

From a basketball standpoint, the two years of Naval duty weren't easy. David didn't always have the chance to work on his own and he just couldn't get into game shape fast enough for the Pan Am Games or the Olympics. But he knew there was very little he could do about it. Like everyone else, he would simply have to wait.

"People I played with in college were out getting better and I wasn't," was the way he put it. "I didn't let it bother me at the time because I couldn't be anywhere else other than where I was. I just resolved to enjoy being in the Navy, which I did.

"In one respect, being in the Navy will help me. Most guys coming into the NBA after college not only have to get used to the pro game, but they also have to get used to the lifestyle of being on their own. I've already had two years of being on my own, so my only adjustment will be to the NBA."

"For me, the biggest thing is to come out and get some confidence so I can play the way I know I'm capable of playing. I have to bring my whole game around, keep learning. There is always something to learn."

David's first step in the learning process was to play in the Spurs' rookie camp. He began looking sharper as the camp progressed. In the final game he was the standout among all those attending, scoring 31 points, grabbing 17 rebounds and blocking 10 shots. Those numbers were vintage Robinson.

Next came the Midwest Rookie Revue, with rookies from the Spurs, Houston,

**David's quickness and agility at Navy often allowed
him to drive to the hoop for an easy slam dunk.**

(Courtesy United States Naval Academy)

David feels just as much at home at the keyboard of a computer as he does on the basketball court.

(Courtesy United States Naval Academy)

On defense, David was just as big a weapon as he was on offense.

(Courtesy United States Naval Academy)

A quick drink during practice and David goes back out on the court to hone his skills.

(Courtesy United States Naval Academy)

David stares down an opposing guard.

(Photo by John Biever)

David is double-teamed and prepares to pass off.

(Photo by John Biever)

Gathering strength during a free throw.

(Photo by John Biever)

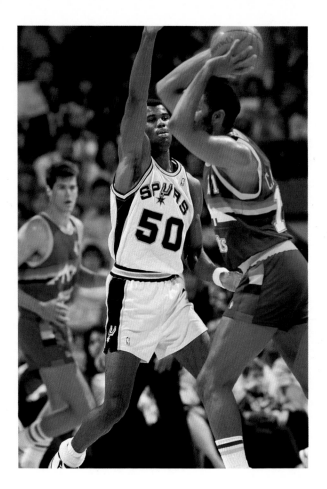

In-your-face defense.

(Photo by John Biever)

Get out of my way!

(Photo by John Biever)

The Spurs' All-Star preparing for a jump ball.

(Photo by John Biever)

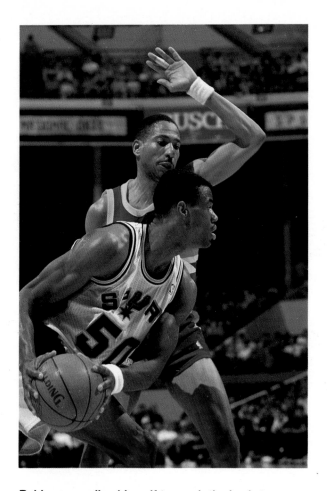

Robinson readies himself to crash the basket.

(Photo by John Biever)

**The Spurs' regulars getting a breather—
Rod Strickland, David Robinson, Sean Elliott and
Terry Cummings.**

(Photo by John Biever)

Robinson skys for a rebound.

(Photo by John Biever)

Robinson snares a rebound and looks downcourt.

(Photo by John Biever)

SLAM-DUNK!!

(Photo by John Biever)

David smiles after a Spurs' victory.

(Photo by John Biever)

Minnesota and Denver playing a round-robin series of games in San Antonio. The fans flocked in mainly to see David Robinson. What they saw convinced them that the team's fortunes would be changing. The Spurs' rookies finished with a 3–0 mark thanks largely to David's 22.7 points, 8.7 rebounds and 4.3 blocks per game.

Next came the Southern California Summer Pro League, which was physical, street rule basketball with very loose officiating. David led his Spurs' teammates to six wins in seven games over 11 grueling days. This time he averaged 25.6 points, 6.4 rebounds and 4.2 blocks. He was subsequently named the league's Most Valuable Player.

"I haven't felt this way in a long time," said an obviously happy Robinson, afterward. "There's a new motivation for me. This is a new challenge and I love challenges. In the summer league I had fun and found the things I needed to work on. I didn't really have any goals out there, although I know the coaches did."

One coach who was impressed was Spurs' assistant Gregg Popovich, who handled the summer league team and watched David carefully. "What impressed me most is the way David responds," Popovich said. "Even when he makes a mistake he looks at the bench and says, 'I know what I did'."

Sound familiar? That was the same thing Art Payne said David had done at Osbourn Park High School his senior year. A player who recognizes his mistakes immediately and has the physical talent can always correct them. No one ever said that David didn't have the physical talent. That was always an asset and something he planned to use in the pros.

"I really don't think I have to change any of my basic skills," he said. "I have to build up my intensity and then utilize my skills, which is something I feel I've always done. I also plan to run all the time and beat my opponent up and down the floor. When I do that, no one can do anything about it. When I run like I can, nobody can run with me."

Confidence was building as training camp approached. Coach Brown and his staff couldn't have been happier. At the same time they knew that they couldn't expect David to be a one-man team, no matter how good he might be. So while David worked at rookie camp and in the summer leagues, the Spurs' brass was also trying to build a solid team to put around him.

At the end of May they traded a pair of front-line players, guard Alvin Robertson and forward Greg Anderson, to the Milwaukee Bucks for 6'9" forward Terry Cummings. Cummings was a 28 year old veteran who had been in the NBA since 1982. An extremely steady player, Terry averaged 23.7 points a game as a rookie for San Diego and had a 22.3 average for his career, going under the 20-point mark only once (19.8). His ability, poise and personality would all help the ballclub and the rookie Robinson.

Step number two came at the end of June. Picking third in the draft, the Spurs tabbed 6'8" forward Sean Elliott of Arizona as their top choice. Though razor thin at 205 pounds, Elliott was not only an All-American but, like David before him, was chosen the college Player of the Year. His 2,555 career points set a PAC 10 record, breaking the mark set years earlier by Lew Alcindor (later known as Kareem Abdul-Jabbar) at UCLA. Some felt Elliott might not be rugged enough for NBA play, but he had credentials to spare.

In July, the Spurs signed free agent Caldwell Jones. At first this pick had people puzzled. Jones was a 14-year NBA survivor. A thin, 6'11" pivotman, Jones was never a star but was known as an outstanding defensive player. At age 39, he didn't have much time left. But for the Spurs, he was a perfect pick. What better player to work with young Robinson, than a guy who knew all the tricks and all the players, and who specialized in defense. If David hadn't been on the way, it's doubtful the Spurs would have signed Jones.

In late August the team made yet another major deal. They sent former top draft choice Johnny Dawkins and journeyman forward Jay Vincent to the Philadelphia 76ers in return for point guard Maurice Cheeks, David Wingate and another player. The key player in the deal was Cheeks.

The speedy backcourtman was a 10-year veteran, perhaps moving downward at age 33. He had been a star point guard since his rookie year and knew how to run a team. He was an outstanding assist man and 12-point career scorer as well. With a number of young players already on the ballclub and several more (Robinson, Elliott) coming in, Coach Brown felt a cool veteran performer like Cheeks was necessary to bring things together.

The season was rapidly approaching. Call it DR day. Training camp was ready to open and perhaps the most anxiously awaited player in franchise history was about to arrive. One thing was certain. He was coming with a purpose.

"I want to be one of the top four centers in the league," David said. "That's what I should be, at the least. I have only one goal and that's to improve each game all year. I don't have number goals, only to rebound and contribute both offensively and defensively.

"But I'm ready. Two years have sometimes seemed like 10. The closer I get, the more anticipation I feel."

7

Rookie of the Year

If David Robinson could achieve his goal of becoming one of the best centers in the National Basketball Association he would be the latest in a line of super big men dating back to the 1940s. However, over the past 50 years, the number of players making up the fraternity of great centers is relatively small.

The first of the great big men was George Mikan, who turned pro in 1946 after a great collegiate career at DePaul. A year later, the 6'10" giant joined the Minneapolis Lakers and became the dominant figure in the NBA's first dynasty. With Mikan in the middle, the old Lakers won five NBA championships in six years.

Though there were a few other players as tall or even taller than Mikan back then, he was the most dominant. Just a tall, clumsy kid when he entered DePaul, Mikan worked on his coordination and his overall game for hours on end. He wound up a powerful player who could score with either hand, clog the middle and rebound better than anybody. He was not nearly as mobile as the pivotmen who came later, but Mikan was the first of the giants who showed he could be a complete basketball player for his time.

Mikan retired after the 1953–54 season and it took just three years for his successor to arrive. He came out of the University of San Francisco, where he led the Dons to a pair of national championships. Bill Russell was a shade under 6'10", not a giant by today's standards, but he played tall.

The most athletic center ever up to that time, Russell was a flyer who could run the floor and had an impeccable sense of timing. He became a tenacious rebounder and maybe the most exciting shot-blocker of his era or any era. If there was a weakness in Russell's game it was his offense. He didn't have a great shot, but still averaged 15 points a game for his career.

The thing Bill Russell did better than any center in history was win. In his 13 years with the Boston Celtics his team became champions 11 times, including an incredible run of eight in a row between 1959 and 1966. Russell, of course, was surrounded by great players such as Bob Cousy, Bill Sharman, Tom Heinsohn, Sam and K.C. Jones, Frank Ramsey and John Havlicek among others. But the big guy made it all work and made opposing players think twice before taking the ball to the hoop. It was Russell who put the "D" in defense in the NBA.

Just three years after Russell arrived in the league along came Wilt Chamberlain. He was a true giant, 7'1", 275 pounds and all athlete. Though some of Wilt's scoring records have since been broken, no one is likely to break the one he set in 1961–62 when he averaged 50 points a game for the old Philadelphia Warriors.

Wilt was perhaps the strongest man ever to play the game and one criticism of him was that he wasn't always mean enough. He could do it all—score, rebound and block shots. Some rate Russell over Wilt because Russell's teams won 11 titles to Chamberlain's two. But no one could ever muscle Wilt on the boards where he remains the NBA's all-time rebounding champ (with Russell a pretty close second).

There were other top centers during the decade of the 1960s, a time often called the Golden Age of Centers. Nate Thurmond, Willis Reed and Jerry Lucas all touched on greatness, though perhaps they were just a notch or two below Russell and Chamberlain. Wes Unseld and Walt Bellamy were two other big men who could turn a game around. So were Bob Lanier, Artis Gilmore and later Bill Walton, who might have been one of the all-time greats had injuries not shortened his career.

In 1969 Lew Alcindor joined the Milwaukee Bucks after an incredible career that produced three national championships at UCLA. He quickly established himself with the Bucks and in his second season led them to an NBA title. The 7'2", 235-pound center continued to excel, eventually changing his name to Kareem Abdul-Jabbar and rewriting a part of the NBA record book. With his famed sky hook, he would become the most prolific scorer in NBA history.

Abdul-Jabbar was traded to the Los Angeles Lakers in 1975 and proceeded to lead his new team to five more NBA titles in the 1980s. Graceful and consistent, a clutch guy when a hoop was needed, Kareem dominated in his own way. He wasn't as tenacious a rebounder as Russell or Chamberlain, but he had the presence of a great center. He was an effective player over a long career that saw him log more games and more minutes than anyone in history.

As David Robinson got set to enter the NBA in 1989, there were two other centers vying to pick up the mantle of Abdul-Jabbar and the greats who came before him. They were Hakeem Olajuwon of the Houston Rockets and Patrick Ewing of the New York Knickerbockers. They were the two premier centers in the game, though neither had yet led his team to a title.

Olajuwon was tough, but graceful, perhaps the best rebounder in basketball. Like David, he had taken up the game of basketball later in life than most since he was born in Nigeria, but he had made up for lost time. A shade under 7 feet, Olajuwon is quickly reaching the point where he can do it all in the NBA.

So can the 7-foot Ewing, as fierce a competitor as there is. A dominating defensive player at Georgetown, Ewing worked to bring his offense up to that level with the Knicks. Extremely tough and athletic, he has become dominating offensively, is a fine shot blocker and intimidator. At the outset of the 1989–90 season, Ewing and Olajuwon were considered a tossup whenever people were trying to decide who was the best center in basketball.

There was one other thing to consider. In the late 1980s and into the 1990s the pro game had changed. It was much more difficult for a center to dominate the way they did in the heyday of Russell and Chamberlain. Guards were no longer 5'11" to 6'3". Some, like the Lakers Magic Johnson were 6'9". In addition, there were many more great all-purpose players in the league. There weren't players like Johnson, Michael Jordan, Clyde Drexler or Scottie Pippen in the 1950s and 1960s. Because other players can do so much more, the center sometimes has to do less.

There aren't as many rebounds to be had because shooting percentages are higher, more players have the talent to go to the hoop, and everyone can slam dunk. Like the other players in today's game, the modern center has to be versatile, especially if he wants to be among the greats. When David came into the league, he already had one very valuable prerequisite. He could run the floor as well as many smaller men.

It was a stronger and quicker David Robinson who came to the NBA from the version who had been at Navy three years earlier. Though he didn't play much during his two-year active hitch, he spent many hours in the weight room working on strength and agility. He was still lean, with thin legs and a 33-inch waist. But his arms and shoulders were extremely muscular. One story said that "his biceps are huge, almost to the point of being grotesque on one so slim." David wasn't coming into the NBA to be pushed around. He was ready to push back.

Top draft choice Sean Elliott didn't sign until about two days before the first exhibition game. He would have some catching up to do. With Cummings, Cheeks and Robinson on board, it was apparent that this was going to be a much different San Antonio Spurs team.

A year earlier, Coach Brown had said publicly that the team roster was not filled with players who would bring the franchise back to respectability. Now, it was different.

"Having Cheeks and Terry is the big thing," the coach said. "The worst thing that could have happened to David would have been to come into the league and not have guys like Cummings, Caldwell Jones and Cheeks around."

The preseason games showed that David was ready. This season was not going to be a repeat of the Pan Am Games or the Olympics. This was a David Robinson who was in shape, primed and ready to go. He showed immediately that he could run with any big man in the league. He also retained that great sense of timing that helped him rebound and block shots. With his speed and shooting touch, it was also obvious that scoring was not going to be a problem for him.

Finally, it was time. Some 15,868 fans jammed the HemisFair Arena in San Antonio to see David and the Spurs take on Magic Johnson and the L.A. Lakers, still one of the best teams in the league. When David's name was announced in the starting lineup he got a huge ovation from the large crowd. They had waited for two years and now would see the results of that wait.

David knew he would be tested early. He came out strong, prepared to establish himself. Three times in the first period alone Laker defenders fouled him as he battled for offensive position underneath. It took just one quarter of action for L.A. to realize it wasn't playing against an ordinary rookie. David would continue to draw fouls and hurt the Lakers by making his free throws.

In the second quarter David was still playing well at both ends of the floor and the game stayed close. Late in the third period, the Spurs had just a 72–70 lead and the Lakers had the ball. Magic Johnson was running the L.A. offense. The Magic man saw an opening and drove the lane looking for a layup. Suddenly, there was David, leaping high in the air and swatting the ball away. It was his first NBA block and it triggered a 6–0 San Antonio run which gave the Spurs a lead they never relinquished. The final score was 106–98. While one game does not a season make, the Spurs had quickly shown one of the NBA's best that they were no longer pushovers. And

David Robinson proved he could play in the NBA. The big guy finished with a team high 23 points, including 11 of 14 from the foul line. He also led both clubs with 17 big rebounds. It was quite a debut.

Magic Johnson, one of the game's all-time greats, paid David the ultimate compliment after the game when he said, "Some rookies are never really rookies. Robinson is one of them."

In the locker room, the reporters and writers gathered around, asking David one question after another. Finally someone said something about the block on Magic and David gave an answer that would become a classic.

"My job is to keep opponents from taking the ball to the hoop with impunity," he said. That one even sent a couple of the scribes running to the dictionary. This was no ordinary, run-of-the-mill jock.

"All the attention I've received is a little bit embarrassing," he said. "All I'm trying to do is make my place in the league."

David also showed that some things hadn't changed from Naval Academy days. Even though he had the enormous task of adjusting to the pros and battling big guys underneath, he still had his usual variety of interests and diversions.

"I feel like I'm growing again, changing, expanding as a person, just like I did in college," he said. "I'm reading a lot, teaching myself to play the piano, even writing some songs."

Two nights later the team lost to Portland, 108–104, despite David's 18 rebounds. He scored 27 and had 13 bounds in a loss at Utah, then came back with 28 points and 11 boards as the Spurs whipped Denver, 122–108. David was establishing himself in a hurry.

By the end of November the team was 8–5 and starting to put things together. There were nine new players on the roster, only three holdovers from the year before. That meant the players had to forge their own chemistry and they were doing it more quickly than anyone had hoped. Cheeks was running the team like the wily veteran he was. Cummings was providing stability and his usual 20-plus point scoring. Willie Anderson continued to play well after a great rookie year, and David was everything the fans had hoped for and more. Only Sean Elliott was struggling a bit, still looking for a feel for the pro game.

Then in December, the ballclub came on strong. Suddenly, the Spurs looked as if they could play with anyone. The month began with a 118–110 victory over Charlotte, with David scoring 32 points and snaring 18 rebounds. It ended with a 101–97 loss to Michael Jordan and the Chicago Bulls. In between, the Spurs won 10 of 11 ballgames to finish December with an 11–2 mark and take over first place in the Midwest Division. At the end of the month the club was 19–7 on the year, the best start ever and a complete flip-flop from a year earlier when they were 7–19 after 26 games.

It was a month in which Terry Cummings was NBA Player of the Week from December 17–24 on the strength of five games in which he scored 29, 26, 29, 28 and 32 points. David was Rookie of the Month for the second straight time and the club had win wins over Houston, Phoenix and Utah, all considered quality teams. In addition, David Robinson was turning heads. His quickness, strength and all-around court presence had not only played a major role in the Spurs' resurgence, but had catapulted him up among the leagues elite pivotmen.

The praise was coming from everywhere. Said New Jersey Nets guard Mookie Blaylock,

"If he's still learning the game, I'd hate to see him when he knows it cold."

Caldwell Jones, the veteran who was brought to San Antonio to help David acclimate to the NBA, put it this way. "He has the talent all us big guys only hope and dream for. No other big guy I've ever see is anywhere as quick and fast as David. That's what really sets him apart."

Center-forward Mark Acres of Orlando said that David shouldn't be talked about in terms of potential. "There's no gonna be about it," Acres said. "David is a great player right now."

The team slowed its pace somewhat in January, but still finished 10–6 for the month. They were now 29–13 for the year with a league best 19–1 record at home. The HemisFair crowds just loved it. They also whipped the Boston Celtics on January 12, winning 97–90 at the Boston Garden, marking the first time they had beaten the Celtics after 20 consecutive losses. The month ended with Terry Cummings getting a career high 52 points against Charlotte and David being named Rookie of the Month for the third straight time.

David had really taken the NBA by storm. In just three months he was already being talked about in the same breath as Ewing and Olajuwon. He had adjusted incredibly fast to the pro game.

"It's been pretty much like I thought it would be," David said. "It's a physical game and a challenging one. At the beginning of the year my fouls used to be ticky-tacky, but I learned real fast to make them count. Up here, you've got to protect your own. I expected physical play, but nothing this bad—guys hanging on you every play, doing anything to stop your shot.

"So it's been tough coming out every night and trying to be great with the kind of competition in the league. I've found the easiest way to get up for every game is to win. So far, we've done all right."

In January, the Spurs went up against Ewing and the Knicks. The final numbers would indicate that the New York center got the better of the confrontation. Ewing finished with 27 points, 12 rebounds and 4 blocks, while David had 20 points, 6 boards and 3 blocks. In the final minutes of a close game, it was David who won the night.

First he hit a fallaway jumper over Ewing's outstretched hand to give the Spurs a 92–90 lead with 1:27 left. At the other end, he anticipated a pass inside, stepped in front of Ewing and stole the ball. A quick outlet pass and the Spurs had a fastbreak that led to a pair of Willie Anderson free throws and a 94–90 lead.

Finally, with the Spurs leading 97–92 and 19 seconds left, he leaped high in the air to reject Ewing's shot off a drive. The final was 101–97, the Spurs on top. David showed all over again that he could play with anyone. By this time the accolades were rolling in.

Don Nelson, coach of the Warriors, said David's game was already complete. "He has everything," Nelson said, "strength, quickness, size, speed. He has all he's going to need. He's phenomenal."

Charles Barkley, the powerful forward of the Philadelphia 76ers and one of the best players in the NBA, couldn't say enough about the rookie. "He's going to be a monster," Barkley said. "He can do it all—play defense, shoot, rebound and block shots. Plus, he's the fastest big man I've ever played against."

Hakeem Olajuwon also recognized that

he now had another real rival to contend with. "He's a great player already," Olajuwon said. "He's quick, he's fast and he's strong. I think he is going to be a great one. For a rookie, he plays with a great deal of confidence. He doesn't hesitate."

Of course, David was quick to return the compliment. When someone asked him about Olajuwon, he said, "He tries to do everything every game, and that makes it difficult to play him. He wants every rebound. He wants to score every point. You can't relax against him. He had a certain pride about him that drives him. He's still hungry."

So was David. At the end of January he was averaging 23.3 points a game, 10th best in the league. His 11.4 rebounding average trailed only Olajuwon (13.4), Barkley (11.8) and Charles Oakley of the Knicks (11.6). He was third in blocks behind—you guessed it— Olajuwon and Ewing. The effect was that the Spurs had the fourth best record in the league.

Not surprisingly, David was chosen to play in the NBA All-Star Game in February. Though he was playing behind Olajuwon on the Western Conference squad, David had a great game. He played 25 minutes, scored 15 points, added 10 rebounds, 2 steals and a block. Though the West lost, 130–113, only Olajuwon with 16 had more rebounds than David.

"I've played with the best there is and did OK," David said, afterward. "I just wanted to fit in. I was a little nervous before the game but when I got in, I felt good and I gained confidence. I know I should control a game night in and night out. Hopefully, I can dominate like I should in the second half of the season."

So David already expected a great deal of himself. He wasn't satisfied. After a two year layoff, he had come back to play just half a season of pro ball and was already being talked about in the same breath as Ewing and Olajuwon. Most people who knew him felt David was going to be a star, but not quite so fast.

"I guess I always thought he would be very good," said his college coach, Pete Herrmann. "But I was surprised at at how well he played after the layoff. David is a very determined person and by talking to him I knew he wanted to go in and establish himself right away his rookie year. The satisfying thing for me as a coach is to see the way he has continued to improve every year he's played basketball. The two years he was off you can toss, but every year he has played a lot of basketball he has continued to improve."

Doug Wojcik, David's point guard at Navy, feels that David has even more motivation for the game now that he's in the pros.

"David wants to be the best," Lt. Wojcik said. "The motivation and commitment is clear to him now. He want to be the best center in the NBA and maybe one of the best of all time. He had that kind of desire.

"In a way, it might be good that he started in the game late and then had that two-year layoff. That way, he didn't take the pounding a lot of guys do. But he's one of those special people who special things happen to. Based on the way it has all gone for him, it's quite an incredible story."

If there were any criticism of David's play his first few months in the pros it was an occasional lapse of concentration that suddenly made him seem to disappear for several minutes during the course of a game. There was a January 8, game against Orlando in which David remained at the defensive end for some 10 San Antonio possessions, which weren't fast breaks. The Spurs lost by 9 even though David wound up with 32 points. But in that game Mark Acres (not exactly a household name) out-rebounded him, 15–10.

The next night he was outplayed by Miami's Rony Seikaly, who scored 21 and had 18 rebounds to David's 20 points and 12 boards. San Antonio managed to win that one, 107–102. Interestingly enough, David's lapse more often than not occurred against the lesser teams and against centers not considered in his class, never against an Olajuwon or Ewing.

"Sometimes I just find myself watching, kind of spacing out," David admitted, with a candor that many professional athletes do not have. "I just don't force myself to go down and get in the action. But don't worry, when it happens Coach Brown lets me know about it.

"At first he didn't yell that much at me," David continued. "But then as he realized I was doing better than he anticipated, he really started to get on me. I'd get 12 rebounds and he'd want 15; I'd block 5 shots and he's want 7. But he should push me because we both know I can get a lot better."

Brown, known as a screamer, needler and

motivator, wanted David to be the best he could be.

"He can be in the Hall of Fame," the coach said. "But when I see Patrick Ewing or Hakeem Olajuwon play, I know David isn't there yet. He's got to decide how badly he wants it, how good he wants to be. He's trying, but I don't know if it will ever happen."

That was the coach's way of getting David to work harder. The occasional lapses notwithstanding, the results spoke for themselves. The Spurs continued to play outstanding basketball. They were en route to another winning month in February when the team made a surprise trade. They sent veteran point guard Maurice Cheeks to the New York Knicks in return for second year point guard Rod Strickland, who had been playing behind Mark Jackson in New York. It seemed odd to disrupt the chemistry of a team that had played so well.

Despite the fact that Cheeks was a wise old head on the court, he was not happy in San Antonio. He had lived in a hotel all season long and asked Coach Brown to try to arrange a trade.

"Mo gave us stability and helped our young

kids develop," said the coach. "He was one of the biggest parts of our turnaround. It's going to take us awhile to adjust to Rod. Maybe 15 games or so; maybe the rest of the season. But in the long run we certainly couldn't get a guy of Rod's ability in the draft. Hopefully, we'll have a young guard who will be part of this team for 10 years."

It was a risky move. Cheeks was the quarterback, the guy who orchestrated the offense and played a solid defense. Strickland was an acknowledged major talent, but he had never run a pro offense for a prolonged period of time. He was also known in some circles as an erratic player who would make mistakes at crucial times by trying to force the action. It's to Brown's credit that he was willing to accommodate an unhappy veteran. The question was how the rest of the team would react.

Though David had been brilliant at times, Cheeks had been a tremendous help to him, as had Cummings. How he would react with a young point guard remained to be seen. Second year man Willie Anderson had also played extremely well, but first year draft choice Sean Elliott was still having trouble acclimating and played well only in spurts. He, too, had benefitted from Cheeks' experience.

To the Spurs' credit, they won four of their first five games after the trade with David named NBA Player of the Week and again tabbed as Rookie of the Month. Even with the change in point guards the team continued to win. They were 11–5 in March, making them 27 games better then their record the year before. A look back at NBA history showed that the greatest one-season turnaround of any team was the Boston Celtics of 1979–80, a club that featured super rookie Larry Bird and finished 32 games better than the year before. The Spurs had a chance to better that mark.

The ballclub not only had a chance to break the turnaround mark, but was also well within striking distance of the franchise record of 53 wins, set in 1982–83 when George Gervin was still the resident superstar. Now the resident superstar was David Robinson. Even Coach Brown admitted that the rookie had made a tremendous impact.

"What's happened is that in one season this has become David's team," the coach said. "He is its heart and soul. I'm not sure he realizes that yet, because everything has happened so quickly. But the more he grows into that role, the better he'll become and the better the team will become."

One player who agreed that the Spurs were David's team was Philadelphia's Charles Barkley. Barkley went so far as to say that he felt the rookie should be the league's Most Valuable Player.

"You have to give Robinson credit," Barkley said. "He has turned things around for the Spurs. If you are judging by which player has improved his team the most, you would have to say that David Robinson is the Most Valuable Player."

Whether he was MVP or not, David had one quality needed to be a Most Valuable Player. He thought about the team first.

"I'm sure people are surprised I've done as much so fast," he said. "But it counts more that the team has also played well. I think any player would tell you that individual accomplishments help your ego, but if you don't win, it makes for a very, very long season."

The Spurs made sure they finished strong. Their 8–3 record in April gave them a club record 56–26 mark for the season and a divisional title. They had won their final seven games in a row to edge out the Utah Jazz by a single game in the Midwest. The Spurs also had the fourth best record in the entire NBA. Only Los Angeles, Portland and Detroit finished with better marks. And yes, the club finished a full 35 games better than the year before, breaking the Celtics turnaround record by three games.

As for David, he had put together a phenomenal rookie year. Not only had he spearheaded the team turnaround, but he had risen spectacularly to be ranked alongside Ewing and Olajuwon as the three best centers in the league. Since David was just a rookie, the consensus was that if he continued to develop, he would eventually surpass the other two.

He finished the season with 1,993 points in 82 games, good for a 24.3 average and 10th best in the league. Ironically, Olajuwon was ninth, having scored just two more points than David all year. Ewing was third in scoring with a 28.6 norm. But neither the Knicks (45–37) nor the Rockets (41–41) had the record San Antonio did.

In rebounding, David had come on to

finish second to Olajuwon with 983 boards and a 12.0 average. He was third in blocked shots with an average of 3.89 a game. Ewing was second with 3.99 and Olajuwon led with 4.59. The big three again. David obviously belonged right up there with them.

He had plenty of help. Cummings averaged 22.4 points a game, while Willie Anderson checked in at 15.7. Cheeks averaged 10.9 points a game before he was traded. Strickland scored at a 14.2 clip after he arrived. Cheeks was getting 6 assists a game with the Spurs, while Strickland averaged 8 a game. So even that controversial late-season trade seemed to pay dividends.

Now David would get his first taste of playoff action. The Spurs would be meeting the Denver Nuggets in the first round, a best-of-five series. They were heavy favorites to win it and judging by the way they had played, had the guns to go all the way. Then just before the playoffs there was an announcement out of NBA headquarters that surprised no one. David Robinson, who had been such a standout in his first pro season, was officially named the NBA's Rookie of the Year.

8

The Playoffs and Beyond

Denver didn't present a major problem. The Nuggets had a 43–39 mark in the regular season, but were mainly a run and shoot team. They scored gobs of points, but so did their opponents. With the Spurs' high-powered offense and David's defense to act as a neutralizer, the San Antonio was the heavy favorite.

The Nuggets fell in three straight as the Spurs had little trouble handling them. The scores were 119–103, 129–120 and 131–120, typical high-scoring donnybrooks that the Nuggets loved to create. Anderson had 27 in the first game, David 31 in the second and Cummings 28 in the third to lead the evenly-balanced scoring. Strickland handed out 31 assists in the three games.

Now came the tough one. The Spurs would be meeting the high-powered Portland Trail Blazers, a team with a 59–23 record during the regular season. The Blazers were led by superstar shooting guard Clyde Drexler, a slick point guard in Terry Porter, a flying forward in Jerome Kersey and a strong, physical center named Kevin Duckworth. This was a very good team.

Before the first game, Portland Coach Rick Adelman said he was thinking of using forward-center Cliff Robinson in the starting lineup, the implication being the quicker Robinson could possibly stay with David better than the slower Duckworth.

"It doesn't matter to me," David said. "I play against whoever. If they think [Cliff Robinson] can play center, then that's great. I don't think he can guard me."

David was showing confidence before the opener. But the matter became unimportant when it was revealed that Duckworth would be sitting out with a broken right hand. Cliff Robinson got the start as the series opened in Portland and it was all Blazers from the

opening tip-off. Portland won it, 107–94, as
David and his teammates looked bad.

Traditionally, playoff basketball has an
intensity not normally seen in the regular
season. David's 9 points, 9 rebounds and only
3 of 11 shooting from the floor might have been
the result of his still adjusting to the heightened
level of play in the playoffs.

"Those kind of games just serve as
reminders sometimes," he said. "Sometimes
it's so easy to forget what you need to do, play
defense and rebound and be active defensively. Anybody who's seen me play all year
knows I don't play like that all the time."

It didn't get much better in the second
game, Portland winning again, 122–112. Coach
Brown had seen enough. He lit into both
David and Terry Cummings, telling them they
were not playing up to the standards they had
set during the regular season. The coach said
he thought David was playing soft inside. He
was also upset with point guard Strickland,
who committed 12 turnovers in the first two
contests.

With the series moving back to the
HemisFair Arena for the third games, David
and the Spurs came to life. The rookie center

regained the toughness that was missing in the first two. In the third game he had what had come to be known as a typical Robinson game. He scored 28 points, collected 8 rebounds and blocked 8 shots. With Cummings adding 19 points and 9 boards the Spurs won it in a walk, 121–98.

Game Four was more of the same, a 115–105 San Antonio victory with David getting 21 points, 10 rebounds and 4 blocks, while Cummings had 35 points and 11 boards. Strickland also came to life, handing out 31 assists and committing just 4 turnovers in the two HemisFair games.

"I think we're starting to play the way we like to play," David said, after the fourth game that evened the series at 2–2. "We're playing more aggressively. Our guards are up on people and we're doing the fundamental things."

The fifth game, back at Portland, was the killer. The teams battled through two overtime periods before the Blazers emerged with a 138–132 victory to take a 3–2 lead in the series. Cummings had 32 points and David 15 rebounds. This was just a superb, very physical basketball game between two fine teams.

It probably set the tone for the sixth game when tempers finally reached a boiling point. Portland star Clyde Drexler was ejected in the third period for throwing a punch at the Spurs' Willie Anderson. Anderson got even by scoring 30 points in a 112–97 San Antonio victory, a game in which David added 13 rebounds and Strickland 12 assists.

That brought it all down to a seventh and deciding game at Portland, the winner advancing to the Conference finals, the loser going home. Like the fifth game, this one was played tight to the vest, a real battle. It was tied at the end of regulation and went into overtime. Neither team would give an inch. Finally, with the scored tied and 30 seconds left the Spurs had the ball. Strickland tried an over-the-head, no-look pass and it was intercepted by Portland. The Blazers pushed the ball upcourt and scored. Seconds later they had a 108–105 victory and advanced to the finals.

"I made a bad decision," Strickland admitted, afterward. "I thought someone was cutting, but in that situation it was a bad play."

In 10 playoff games David averaged 24.3 points, 12 rebounds and 4 blocks a game, remarkably close to his regular season stats.

So he was consistent. The biggest disappointment was the team's defeat.

The other Western Conference finalist was the Phoenix Suns, a team that defeated the L.A. Lakers, the team of the 1980s with five championships. Phoenix Coach Cotton Fitzsimmons felt that no team would be able to win five titles in a decade during the 1990s. There was just too much parity, too many good teams. But Fitzsimmons said there was one team that had a chance to dominate and for a particular reason.

"The only team that has a chance [to dominate] in the '90s is San Antonio, because of David Robinson."

So despite the playoff loss, David had won the respect of everyone. His accomplishments in his first pro season were as good as any player in the game. Of the centers, only Russell, Chamberlain and Abdul-Jabbar came into the league with the same kind of impact. Even Olajuwon and Ewing needed a period of adjustment.

After the season, there were more accolades. Besides being Rookie of the Year, David was also on the All-Rookie Team, was third team All-NBA (behind Olajuwon and Ewing), second team All-Defense and won the Schick Award for Player of the Year.

Though his third team All-NBA selection put him behind Olajuwon and Ewing, an interesting rating system, called the TENDEX, said something difference. The TENDEX ratings were released monthly, then tabulated for the year. They were calculations based on 10 statistical categories.

Not surprisingly, Chicago Bulls great Michael Jordan had the top TENDEX rating for the year, an .871. Tied for second were power forward Karl Malone of Utah and David Robinson, each with an .854 rating. Olajuwon was next at .851 and then Ewing at .829. So in the eyes of the TENDEX system, figured mathematically, David Robinson was the league's best center in 1989-90, and close to being its best player.

It was a busy off season for David. He had to spend several weeks fulfilling his Naval reserve commitment. There was also a huge demand for personal appearances and an ever growing role as a commercial spokesman. It didn't take him long to become a favorite with the kids and with fans in general. Like superstars Michael Jordan and Magic Johnson,

David was courteous and personable in nearly every situation and a tremendous spokesman and representative for the league.

His commercials also began multiplying rapidly, the ad campaigns referring to him as "Mr. Robinson," and taking advantage of his many off-court interests, portraying him as more than just another jock. His academic achievements and clean-cut image were also part of the ad campaigns.

"The 'Mr. Robinson' persona is perfect for him because he is such a nice guy off the court," said Melinda Gable, a spokesman for the shoe company that David represented.

David was very careful in cultivating a positive image. He believes that athletes in the public eye should be role models.

"I don't think a lot of guys take it [their image as role models] as seriously as they should," David said. "But to me it's very important. The influence you can have on kids is one of the best things about the position I'm in and I spend a lot of time with them. I go out and talk to as many kids as I can, trying to help them and give them a little boost."

He may have been in a fishbowl, but David Robinson was thriving in it. Just four short years earlier, David had completed his freshman year at Navy, a tall, thin freshman who still didn't know the fundamentals of the game. He probably never envisioned a professional basketball career then. In fact, he admitted that at first basketball was not something he loved.

"I didn't have a whole lot of feeling toward basketball," he admitted. "I was just a tall kid and I didn't feel natural doing it and didn't have a particular gift for it. I thought it was just a recreational thing. I never thought this was something I was going to be successful at. It just worked out that way."

Now he was one of the biggest stars in all of sports. Yet with all his other activities he still prepared arduously for his second pro season. There was still a lot to learn.

"If you're going to be a great musician," David said, "you have to have all the basics down and go from there. But with basketball, I don't really think I have all the basics down yet. There are so many things I feel like a need to learn. My effort and athletic ability help me overcome some of the things I don't do as well right now, but soon I'm going to know how to do those things. And I'm going to be a lot better."

David continued to claim that his best asset was his ability to run the floor. "I do much better in transition and when I'm driving the ball to the basket," he said. "When I go into a game, I think, 'Run, David, move your feet'. I really don't have anything past that, to be honest."

In the eyes of others, he had plenty. Phoenix Suns coach Cotton Fitzsimmons said that David was "the greatest impact player the league has seen since Kareem Abdul-Jabbar." After watching David perform over the first several months of 1990-91, the same Fitzsimmons claimed that the Spurs' center had already surpassed Michael Jordan, Magic Johnson and Larry Bird as the game's most imposing player. "They're all MVP's," Fitzsimmons said, "but this guy is more."

Some felt that the Spurs had a shot to go all the way to the top in the new season, David's second. Even though Sean Elliott was beginning to look much better and veteran guard Paul Pressey came from Milwaukee via a trade, there were problems before the season even began. Both Willie Anderson and Rod Strickland were sidelined with stress fractures in the left leg. Anderson was slated to miss three weeks, Strickland at least 10 days.

"We knew we had a scrambled lineup," David said. "It's been a little different, but everyone has been playing well."

There was no reason to worry as the season opened. Strickland surprised everyone by coming back in just the third game and promptly scoring a career high 27 points in a 111–110 victory over Houston. Anderson, however, had to go on the injured list. As for David, after four games he was averaging 30.5 points, shooting 63.6 percent from the floor and had blocked 16 shots. He was looking better than ever.

It wasn't long before David began putting together some very big games. His first was a 40-point, 14-rebound, 5-block outing against Phoenix, a game the Spurs won, 128–114. No wonder Phoenix Coach Fitzsimmons couldn't say enough about him. And David was feeling pretty good, too.

"I feel a lot better about myself," he said. "I also feel better about the team and I hope part of that is because I'm a better player."

It was. In fact, the club was looking so

good that one writer felt that "once guard Willie Anderson returns from the injured list, no team in the Midwest Division will be able to keep up with San Antonio."

In early December the club lost two important games, to Portland (the hottest team in the league) and then the Lakers during a west coast trip. In the Laker game, the Spurs were held to a season-low 80 points and shot just 38 percent from the floor. The good news was that Elliott had averaged 19.7 points in the team's last three games, while the bad news was that veteran forward Sidney Green, picked up before the season, was lost from four to six weeks with bone spurs in his ankle.

After the 17-point loss to the Lakers, Coach Brown berated his team in the locker room. "It was upsetting and an awful effort on our part. We just talked about what it takes to be a championship team. We've got to become a team. We didn't act like a team."

Toward the end of December the Spurs were leading the Midwest again and were considered one of five teams (Portland, Boston, Chicago and Detroit the others) with the best chance to win the NBA title. But injuries were a continuing problem. When

Willie Anderson finally returned and was trying to play himself into shape, Terry Cummings went down with a knee injury.

The Spurs won a big game against Houston, 96–95, with David playing rival Hakeem Olajuwon to a standoff. Olajuwon had 20 points, 14 rebounds and 3 blocks, while David had 18 points, 13 boards and 8 big blocks.

"If they [Robinson and Olajuwon] are a dead heat, then I'm really thrilled," said Coach Brown. "Olajuwon is in his seventh season while David's only been in the league for 100 games. But I really feel that David is different from any center. He has unbelievable speed. I remember when Kareem [Abdul-Jabbar] would dribble to half court and everybody in the Forum would stand up. I've seen this kid dribble the length of the floor as if he were a guard. We take it for granted, because sometimes when you're watching him he plays like he's six feet tall."

Through 28 games of the season the Spurs were looking good. Despite the injuries that plagued them in the early going the team had compiled a 21–7 record, tied for third best in the entire NBA. The club had also played the majority of its games on the road. As for David, he was dominating. He was leading the league with 4.12 blocks a game, was second to Olajuwon with 12.5 rebounds, and was eighth in scoring with an average of 25.4. The other big plus was Sean Elliott, who had grown from an unsure rookie to a solid second-year player averaging more than 15 points a game.

It was David who continued to be the real head-turner. In a game with the Hawks he had 35 points and 16 rebounds, prompting Atlanta's electric superstar, Dominique Wilkens, to say, "They talk about Ewing and Olajuwon, but I see [David] doing things they can't do."

During a four-game stretch in mid-January, David averaged 32.7 points, 15.5 rebounds and 7.2 blocks shots. If those aren't dominating numbers, then dominating numbers don't exist. More often rival coaches were talking about the way the big guy took games into his own hands.

"His presence is such a factor," said Orlando coach Matt Guokas. "He does such a good job clogging the middle. He distorts your whole game."

Paul Westhead, coach of the run-and-gun

Denver Nuggets, could only watch helplessly as David scored 31 points against his team, adding 4 blocks. Of David's points, 24 came on dunks as the Spurs won by 14. "Robinson turned things around almost single-handedly," said Westhead. "He was certainly in the middle of a dunkathon. On a couple of plays he blocked a shot, outletted the ball, filled the lane and then finished off with a dunk. Most guys just block and outlet, but [David] is double jeopardy."

With the All-Star break approaching, the Spurs continued to chase Pacific Division leader Portland for the best record in the NBA and David continued to play well. Olajuwon was out of action with an eye injury and David was outscoring, out-rebounding and outblocking Ewing. He was looking like the NBA's best center in 1990–91.

It wasn't surprising when David was named a starter for the West in the All-Star Game. The TENDEX rating at the time of the game showed him with the highest rating in the entire league, a .942 mark. The Bulls' Michael Jordan was next at .903. So according to TENDEX, David was the best player in the NBA. In addition, he was the leading All-Star vote-getter in the Western Division.

After 41 games, the halfway mark, the Spurs had a record of 30–11, two games better than they had the year before. Portland was still tops with 34–7, while the Celtics were 31–10, the Lakers 30–11 and the Bulls 29–12. The defending champion Pistons were 28–13, while the Suns and Jazz were both at 27–14. So there were many quality teams. The Spurs continued to have problems with injuries. Now it was Strickland again and Cummings. Both were lost with broken hands. So David would be asked to carry an even larger load.

On top of everything else, there were disturbing world events taking place that could possibly affect David's immediate future. War had broken out in the Persian Gulf and the United States was rushing a huge force into action. Since David was in the reserves, there was a chance he could be called to active duty. If it happened, he would probably be assigned to the Naval Facilities Engineering Command in Washington.

Fortunately, David was never called. Because of his Naval Academy background, he was asked about the war wherever he went. It was as if he was the NBA's unofficial spokesman for the Gulf War, known as Operation Desert Storm. David told the media repeatedly that he would gladly go if called. That was unlikely because of his height. It obviously disturbed him though that many of his former classmates and friends from the Academy were involved.

"The whole thing was pretty intense for me," David said. "When I turned on the news and heard the guys on the first planes had left that morning for a bombing run over Baghdad, my stomach just dropped. I imagined those guys must be scared to death. The whole thing made playing basketball seem insignificant."

But David had to stay focused. He had problems with distractions at Navy and early in his career, and with the Gulf War going on it could have been something else to take his mind off the game. David talked about how he was sometimes distracted and why he felt it could happen sometimes.

"I get a lot of enjoyment out of different things," he said. "Music, people, basketball. But if I'm thinking about something else in a game, I drift. If I come into a game focused, I stay focused. Magic [Johnson] was focused for years because basketball was his main

interest. Now he's trying to develop other
interests. I came into the league with other
interests and had to learn to focus on basketball.

"Life is a learning process. I have to learn
to sacrifice things for basketball, but I can't
lose my identity. I have to continue to be
happy."

By late February, David had taken over
the league rebounding lead from the injured
Olajuwon and continued to lead in blocks. His
scoring average was up to 26.1, due partially
to the injuries to other players. More of the
burden was being put on David and he was
responding. Cummings returned to the lineup
at the end of the month, but Strickland was
still out and the team missed his floor
generalship.

The beginning of March was a rough time
for the Spurs. They had won just four of 12
after the Strickland injury and watched as
Utah took over first place in the division.
Among the losses were a pair to Boston and
New York in which the Spurs blew leads of 17
and 18 points, something the top teams rarely
do. Finally, a big win over Portland turned the
team around again.

"I felt like we had a lot of problems and weren't working together very well," David said. "In fact, it looked kind of bleak. But we turned it around [beating Portland] and the confidence is back."

With 24 games remaining, the Spurs and Jazz were in a virtual tie. San Antonio was 39–19 and the Jazz 40–20. The Celtics, Bulls, Trailblazers and Lakers all had better records, as did the Suns at 42–19. It looked as if the Spurs would need that number one spot to get the home court advantage in the playoffs. They kept running neck and neck, however, with the Jazz.

By mid-March, David still had the best TENDEX rating of any player in the league. Strickland was almost ready to return from his broken hand and the Spurs were 21–5 when all five starters were healthy and in the lineup. A look at the stats showed that only Robinson and Elliott had played all 63 games to date. Cummings had played 48, Anderson 56, Strickland just 39, Paul Pressey 57, Sidney Green 49. Time lost to injury had definitely hurt the team.

By the end of March the race in the Midwest Division had become a three-team affair. The Houston Rockets had gotten back into contention during Hakeem Olajuwon's stay on the injured list. It was a case of a team pulling together with their biggest star out, proving once more that it was still a team game. Two games separated Utah, San Antonio and Houston.

With all five starters healthy, the Spurs regained the division lead by mid-month. David averaged 32.8 points, 16.3 rebounds and 4.3 blocks during a four-game surge the second week of the month. The team was feeling pretty good about itself, but guard Willie Anderson made an observation that could have been a prediction of the team's postseason play.

"Our half-court offense is pretty good, but we've still got to work on it," Anderson said. "The playoffs are more of a half-court game, not the up-tempo game that we like to play. We've got to improve on that."

It was true. With a center as fast as David, the Spurs loved to run. In games against teams that like to slow the offense and keep it in the half court and also had the ability to stifle the Spurs' break, things were always tougher. Remember playoff basketball is a different game—tighter and tougher. The Spurs had, however, played well in the playoffs the season before. That should have been valuable experience.

The three teams continued to battle. With a week remaining, San Antonio was at 51–26, Utah a half game back at 51–27, while Houston was one back at 50–27. It couldn't get much closer than that. If there happened to be a tie for the division crown between San Antonio and Utah, however, the Jazz would win it because they had taken the season series from the Spurs, 3–2. So no one could relax.

In the final week the Spurs took four of five games to win the division with a 55–27 mark. It was their second straight divisional title and their record was just one game below that of the season before. The Jazz finished a game behind with Houston three back. Had they been healthier, the Spurs undoubtedly would have won it more easily. They had players miss a total of 108 games, including 46 by the starters.

"I'm very proud of this team," Coach Brown said. "With all the injuries and everything else that's happened, we've done as well, if not better, than we could have expected."

As for David, it had been another brilliant season. He played every game for the second year in a row, this time averaging 25.6 a game, finishing ninth in the league in scoring. His top effort was a 43-point performance. He also led the league in rebounds, averaging 13 a game with a high of 23. In addition he was second in blocks with a 3.90 per game average, twice nailing 11 in a single game and he was ninth in field goal percentage (55.2) making him the only player in the league to be in the top ten in four separate categories. No wonder he jumped to the head of the class as the center on the All-NBA Team and was named to the first team All-Defense. There was little argument.

Now it was on to the playoffs where the Spurs would have to meet the Golden State Warriors in the opening round. The Warriors were led by a trio of high scorers—Chris Mullin (25.7), Milt Richmond (23.9) and Tim Hardaway (22.9). None of the three was taller than 6'6" and the Warriors didn't have a bonafide center. Even though the teams had split four games in the regular season, the Spurs were heavy favorites.

All five Spurs' starters scored in double

figures for the year. Cummings was second to David, averaging a career low 17.6. Then came Elliott at 15.9, Anderson at 14.4 and Strickland at 13.8. It was important they stay healthy because the bench wasn't real strong. What happened in the playoffs, though, not only exposed some inherent weakness in the Spurs, but also pointed up the changing nature of the professional game.

Coach Don Nelson of the Warriors knew he didn't have a big man who could match David and he didn't want to try. Instead, he built his game plan around his three stars—Mullin, Richmond and Hardaway—and hoped by using speed and ball movement, he could take David and the Spurs out of their game.

Jim Peterson, one of the Warrior centers who would have to battle David, said his coach "wanted to go with more mobile guys and keep David guessing on the defensive end. He wanted to make sure this wasn't a 'big guy' series."

Speed and mobility made the first game a high-scoring affair. When it ended, San Antonio had a 130–121 victory and almost everyone figured things were going according to script. The Warriors were giving them a battle, but it was expected that they didn't have the firepower to match David and the Spurs. In the second game, things suddenly changed. The San Antonio offense didn't have balance and Golden State took advantage. Mullin, Richmond and Hardaway continued to use their speed and mobility and were hitting the open shots. When it ended they had tied the series with a 111–98 victory.

It was in the third game when people began to realize that the Spurs were having trouble coping with the Warriors style. Golden State won a tough, 109–106, decision in which they hit the clutch shots down the stretch. Now the Spurs were in trouble, trailing 2-1 in a best-of-five series. David had been playing well through the first three. He had 85 points, 40 rebounds and was shooting a devastating 70 percent from the floor.

Yet in the fourth game not even David's presence made any difference. In fact, it was David's poorest game offensively and his teammates just couldn't pick up the slack. The big guy scored just 18 points and the Warriors won the game, 110–97, eliminating the Spurs from the playoffs and maybe sending them back to the drawing board. David, for one, was devastated.

"We just let them get aggressive and take the game away from us," he said. "This is tough. I don't feel I fulfilled my responsibility. I have to take a lot of responsibility for this team. I like to think I have an impact on the team, so you like to play well in these games. It's very disappointing."

Except for perhaps the final game, David had played well. In the playoffs he averaged 25.8 points a game, got 54 rebounds and blocked 15 shots. His numbers were very close to his regular season stats, showing once again his consistency. But there were to be questions about some of the other starters. Was Terry Cummings on the downside? Would Rod Strickland avoid injury and find consistency in his game? Would Sean Elliott become the star he was in college?

There were other questions, as well. For one thing, the two other so-called dominant centers in the game, Patrick Ewing and Hakeem Olajuwon, also saw their teams eliminated in the first round of the playoffs. Was the game changing so that a dominant center no longer guaranteed winning? After all, the Detroit Pistons had won the last two NBA titles with journeyman Bill Laimbeer in the middle. And the Chicago Bulls would win in 1990–91 with an aging Bill Cartwright at center.

"You can't win with one guy anymore," said Philadelphia's Charles Barkley. "You need a supporting cast. Coaching is too good these days to let one big superstar beat you."

Willis Reed, who had been a dominant center with the New York Knicks in the early 1960s, didn't feel the center should take the blame for his team's failings.

"It's not fair to say that a center didn't do the job," Reed said. "Maybe he doesn't have good enough players around him."

Philadelphia Coach Jim Lynam felt that quick, double-teaming defenses have help take away the importance of the dominating center.

"I used to watch Wilt Chamberlain play quite often," Lynam said. "I remember one night when he scored 78 points. Yet how many times did the other team double-team him? Hardly ever. Defenses do it all the time now. The defenses played differently then."

And Charles Barkley added yet another possible reason. "Not too many guys can do what I can do at 6'4½" and 250 pounds," he said. "I can play with power, and yet I'm quick and I can get up and down the floor. Most centers can't do that."

The one who can is David Robinson. If the game is indeed changing, and there are indications that it is, then David may well be the center of the nineties. Of the three so-called superstar centers, David is the one who can run the floor the best. He's the most mobile and the quickest. In addition, he has only played two seasons in the league. He will get better. With the right kind of team around him, it's widely acknowledged that David could lead his team to several championships.

That, certainly, is David's goal. Besides being a great basketball player, one who is constantly striving to improve, David is also representative of the new breed of athlete, someone whose horizons extend far beyond the hardwood of the basketball floor. That was never more in evidence than in what David did immediately after the Spurs were eliminated from the playoffs by the Warriors.

He appeared at the Gates Elementary School in San Antonio and helped initiate a fifth-grade class at the school into the I Have a Dream Foundation. In sponsoring the class, David committed to helping provide scholarships for those students in the class who graduate from high school and qualify to attend a university associated with the foundation.

Appearing with David was the founder of the organization, Eugene Lang. Lang told the students and their parents that "from this day on your life will never be the same. About 10,000 students, each of whom has a dream and knows that dreaming is possible—they now believe in themselves."

As for David, it was something he had wanted to do for some time. "This is really a bright spot for me," he told the audience. "We finished up the [basketball] season kind of on a bad note, so this is really the first good positive thing that has happened to me since the season ended. I hope you don't mind, but I'm going to think of you guys as my kids."

It was just another example of the all-around person David Robinson has become. He is not only one of pro basketball's best players, but also one of the NBA's best spokesmen. He has shown that it is possible to have a variety of interests and pursuits while still excelling and improving in your sport. And he has handled his growing fame and commitments with grace and dignity. It's hard to find anyone who says a bad word about him.

Perhaps the person most proud of David's achievements is his father, Ambrose Robinson. He has seen his son grow as an athlete, as a person and as a role model. "I'm just so pleased that David has had such an impact on people's lives, especially the kids," his father said.

Ambrose Robinson has also commented on the tough part of David's sudden fame— people's expectations and a complete loss of privacy.

"There have been times where David has said, 'I never realized it would be like this'," said his father. "That's why at first I was a little antsy about how David would react to all this—the money and the attention. I'm happy he's handled it the way he has. He's the same person. I know he's not snotty. What you see is what you get."

And that's what scares the guys who have to play against David Robinson on the basketball court. What they see is what they get. And that is very close to the best there is.

DAVID ROBINSON
COLLEGE & PRO STATISTICS

United States Naval Academy

Season	G	FGs	Pct	FTs	Pct	Reb	Blks	Pts	Avg
1983-84	28	86	62.3	42	57.5	111	37	214	7.6
1984-85	32	302	64.4	152	62.6	370	128	756	23.6
1985-86	35	294	60.7	208	62.8	455	207	796	22.7
1986-87	32	350	59.1	202	63.7	378	144	903	28.2
Totals	127	1,032	61.3	604	62.7	1,314	516	2,669	21.0

San Antonio Spurs

Season	G	FGs	Pct	FTs	Pct	Reb	Blks	Pts	Avg
1989-90	82	630	53.1	613	73.2	983	319	1,993	24.3
1990-91	82	754	55.2	592	76.2	1,063	320	2,101	25.6
Totals	164	1,444	54.2	1,205	74.7	2,046	639	4,094	25.0

Playoffs

Season	G	FGs	Pct	FTs	Pct	Reb	Blks	Pts	Avg
1989-90	10	89	53.3	65	67.7	120	40	243	24.3
1990-91	4	35	68.6	33	86.8	54	15	103	25.8
Totals	14	124	61.0	98	77.3	174	55	346	25.1

About the Author

Bill Gutman has been a freelance writer for 20 years. In that time he has written well over 100 books, many of them in the sports field and covering all major sports. Biography has always been a special favorite. His very first book was a biography of Pistol Pete Maravich, and one of his most recent is an autobiography of former New York Giants baseball star Bobby Thomson, as well as a recreation of the 1951 pennant race between the Giants and Brooklyn Dodgers. Mr. Gutman currently lives in Poughquag, New York, with his wife and two stepchildren.